DOREEN VIRTUE

Removing New Age from Your Home

A Checklist & Guide to Getting Occult Influences out of the Christian Home

First published by Amazing Grace 2025

Copyright © 2025 by Doreen Virtue

All rights reserved. No part of this publication may be reproduced, stored or transmitted in any form or by any means, electronic, mechanical, photocopying, recording, scanning, or otherwise without written permission from the publisher. It is illegal to copy this book, post it to a website, or distribute it by any other means without permission.

Christian Standard Bible (CSB)

Publisher: Holman Bible Publishers

Copyright: © 2017 by Holman Bible Publishers

Fair Use Statement: The verses in this work are used under the Fair Use copyright law.

English Standard Version (ESV)

Publisher: Crossway

Copyright: © 2001 by Crossway

Fair Use Statement: The verses in this work are used under the Fair Use copyright law.

King James Version (KJV)

Publisher: Various publishers (original 1611 edition is public domain, but modern editions are published by different houses like Thomas Nelson or Cambridge University Press)

Copyright: Public domain for the original 1611 edition, but modern editions may have specific copyright for certain elements (e.g., introduction, commentary)

Fair Use Statement: The verses in this work are used under the Fair Use copyright law.

New American Standard Bible (NASB)

Publisher: The Lockman Foundation

Copyright: © 1995 by The Lockman Foundation

Fair Use Statement: The verses in this work are used under the Fair Use copyright law.

New International Version (NIV)

Publisher: Zondervan (a division of HarperCollins)

Copyright: © 2011 by Biblica, Inc.™

Fair Use Statement: The verses in this work are used under the Fair Use copyright law.

New King James Version (NKJV)

Publisher: Thomas Nelson

Copyright: © 1987 by Thomas Nelson

Fair Use Statement: The verses in this work are used under the Fair Use copyright law.

The New Living Translation (NLT)

Publisher: Tyndale House Publishers, Inc.

Copyright © by Tyndale House Publishers, Inc.

Fair Use Statement: The verses in this work are used under the Fair Use copyright law.

First edition

This book was professionally typeset on Reedsy.
Find out more at reedsy.com

Contents

Chapter 1: No Fellowship with Darkness	1
Chapter 2: Reducing Spiritual Warfare in Your Home	11
Chapter 3: New Age and Idolatrous Statues & Artwork to...	16
Checklist for Finding and Removing Idolatrous Statues and...	32
Chapter 4: New Age Divination Tools to Remove from Your Home	34
Checklist for Finding and Removing New Age Divination Tools...	44
Chapter 5: New Age Jewelry to Remove from Your Home	46
Checklist for Removing New Age Jewelry from Your Home	57
Chapter 6: New Age Clothing to Remove from Your Home	59
Checklist for Removing New Age Clothing from Your Home	77
Chapter 7: New Age and False Gospel Books to Remove from...	79
Checklist for Removing New Age Books from Your Home	111
Chapter 8: Conjuring Tools of Wicca, Witchcraft, and the...	113
Checklist for Removing Conjuring Items from Your Home	118
Chapter 9: Deleting Digital New Age Items	120
Chapter 10: Bible Verses to Encourage You	135
Chapter 11: As for Me and My House, We will Serve the Lord	140

About the Author 144
Also by Doreen Virtue 146

Chapter 1: No Fellowship with Darkness

My home looked like a New Age metaphysical store before God saved me in 2017. Almost every room was stuffed with statues and paintings of Hindu and Buddhist deities, crystal pendulums, occult books, divination cards, yoga mats, and clothing with new age symbols. My phone was also filled with new age apps about astrology, divination, and eastern meditation.

Perhaps your home isn't as extreme as mine was, yet you still may be knowingly or unknowingly harboring new age or occult items in your home. Ever since God opened my eyes and saved me in 2017 as I was reading the Bible, I've been warning about new age deception.

Many professing Christians have told me that they didn't realize that they owned new age materials. They were horrified to learn that they were unknowingly involved with new age practices. In this book, we'll do a deep dive into some items you may have in your home that are new age, new thought, or occultic in nature.

The Narrow Path

Jesus told us that He is the way, the truth, and the life. No one can come to Father God without Jesus (John 14:6).

We can't co-mingle or blend other religions and spiritual paths with Christianity, because Christianity is a narrow path. We can love people of other religions and traditions. We should pray for them and seek to share the Gospel with them. But we shouldn't try to adopt their religious or spiritual customs, beliefs or symbols - especially into our homes.

The bottom line is that Jesus died for the sins of paganism, idolatry, sorcery, witchcraft, and divination. Why would we want to glorify any of those sins with items in our home?

God's Word warns us to not open our homes to false teachers or teachings (2 John 1:10). So, we shouldn't open our homes to false teachings within books or other items related to false teachings. As parents, we also need to protect our children from these influences.

Beyond Decluttering

We hear a lot these days about decluttering, yet removing new age and occultic items from your home is light years beyond getting rid of clutter. It's removing spiritual garbage from your home.

In the new age, we were obsessed with "clearing our space," meaning that we wanted to banish "negative energy" from our surroundings. To do this, I was involved with a form of spiritual housekeeping called "feng shui" that teaches that clutter disrupts the "energy flow" of a home. In feng shui, we'd rearrange, redecorate, and add and remove certain objects for protection and to "manifest" our desires.

When I toured with a famous psychic, he taught me a method of visualizing spiritual energy grids around the stages where we gave seminars and audience readings. Another new age practitioner made his own sprays made from essential oils mixed with ground-up crystals, as his way of "clearing the energy."

Yet, those new age efforts couldn't yield the peace that we sought - they actually ensnared us further in deception. Only through our faith in Jesus and yielding our life to Him as our Lord and Savior can we be

CHAPTER 1: NO FELLOWSHIP WITH DARKNESS

saved and find eternal peace.

My Testimony

After my husband and I were saved in late 2017, I went through our home with large contractor-size trash bags and prayed for the Holy Spirit to guide me in disposing of anything that was unbiblical. My husband rented a commercial sized dumpster and we filled it to the top with pagan statues, artwork, jewelry, books, cards, clothing, and other items that don't belong in a Christian home.

I knew that I couldn't sell or donate these items, because I didn't want to pass along the deception to others. I already felt horrible that in the new age, I'd taught others about the deception that I was unknowingly under.

I was raised in the new thought church of Christian Science, and my parents had raised me to believe that our thoughts create our reality. In the 1990's, I was invited to speak and tour with a traveling new age mind-body-spirit conference called the Whole Life Expo. It was primarily through touring with this conference that I segued from new thought to new age.

From the 1990's until God saved me in 2017, I toured as a new age teacher and appeared on talk shows such as Oprah, The View, CNN, and others. My publisher and event producers treated my husband and I like rock stars, with first class travel and accommodations. I soon was listed in the annual Watkins list as one of the top 15 most influential spiritual teachers in the world. At one time, I boasted about this, but now I cringe because I passed along the deception with which I'd been born and raised.

I had paranormal visions and experiences since childhood. I now realize they were caused by demons who take advantage of sensitive lonely children who aren't under the cover of a biblically solid family who prays for their spiritual safety.

The visions I received on behalf of other people were a mixture of accurate messages mixed with new age and new thought deception. Eventually, I became a professional stage psychic who gave readings to audiences, on television, and on radio.

Since people said that my new age work comforted them, I thought that God approved of my work. I had no idea that giving readings and other new age practices were condemned, until I finally read the entire Bible. Plus, my new thought upbringing had brainwashed me into believing that we humans were all "good people" and that there was no such thing as sin or hell. Praise God that He allowed me to live long enough to be saved out of that dangerous madness!

I always thought of myself as a Christian, having been raised in "Christian Science" (it's a false gospel and not Christian, but I didn't know that at the time) where we attended church twice weekly and read the KJV Bible out of context daily. So, I would listen to Christian sermons on the radio throughout my life. On January 15, 1995 I heard a sermon about false prophets that convicted me and led me to study the Bible. Two and one-half years later, as I read Deuteronomy 18:9-12, God opened my eyes that I had sinned against our holy God. That's when I repented, gave my life to Jesus as my Lord and Savior, and left the new age.

Jesus came to earth as fully God and fully man and lived a sinless life so that He could take the punishment that we all deserve since we've all sinned (Romans 3:23). He died on the cross to save our souls, and He was buried for three days as prophesied, until He bodily rose from the dead. Jesus conquered sin and death on our behalf, and those who believe in the Gospel have their sins forgiven and can have eternal life with Jesus in Heaven. Those who reject the Gospel are judged for their sins and cast into eternal torment.

CHAPTER 1: NO FELLOWSHIP WITH DARKNESS

Removing Paganism and Idolatry from Our Homes

We aren't saved by our good works, yet once we're saved we desire to please and obey God. Getting the idols and other pagan items out of our homes is obedience to God. I threw out thousands of dollars worth of artwork, books, statues, jewelry and clothing. We see a similar process with new Christians burning their expensive sorcery materials in Acts 19:19.

With each garbage bag that we tossed into the dumpster, there was a sense of relief. I'd been experiencing horrible insomnia-producing spiritual warfare ever since I left the new age to follow Jesus. It's normal for Christians to be oppressed by demons who try to discourage their witness. Yet, there was a definite reduction in spiritual warfare after the dumpster company towed away all of that garbage.

New age items aren't "possessed" by demons, but they can definitely be an entry-point to spiritual warfare. The Bible describes sin as being an element that leads to demonic oppression, and it's a sin to be involved in new age practices and have new age items.

In addition, these new age items can be a temptation for some people. It's just like an alcoholic shouldn't keep alcohol in his home so he's not tempted to relapse.

When a professing Christian has new age items in her home, it could cause someone else to stumble into new ageism. You remember when the Apostle Paul discussed in 1 Corinthians 8 and 10 how the meat that was prayed over in pagan temples could be redeemed and eaten by Christians? Well, he never said that the pagan temples or the pagan prayers could be redeemed. Those unredeemable pagan prayers and temples are analogous to new age practices.

Paul also said that he'd never eat or drink anything that could cause someone else to stumble from his example. Well, if a person visits a Christian home and sees pagan statues, artwork, books, or other items in that home . . . it could cause her to think that it's fine for Christians to have pagan items. She may buy similar pagan items as a result. Children in the home may also be influenced by seeing their parents use new age items. In my case, when I'd visit my paternal grandmother, I used her divination tools which influenced me to believe that divination is fine for Christians since she was a church-going Presbyterian. So, there are many reasons to get the new age items out of our home!

"Have nothing to do with the fruitless deeds of darkness, but rather expose them." Ephesians 5:11

Besides, why would we want to have any item in our home that is amongst the sins that our Lord and Savior Jesus died on the cross for? He suffered and died to save our souls from the punishment that we all deserve for the sins that we've all committed (Romans 3:23), and that includes the sins of idolatry, divination, sorcery, and witchcraft that are inherent within new age practices.

The bottom line is that Christianity and new age items cannot commingle. Christianity is about glorifying, submitting to, trusting, loving, and obeying God. New age is self-obsessed and is about affirming and elevating the self as a coping mechanism. New age practices and items violate the Bible's commandments against idolatry, divination, sorcery, and witchcraft.

Even though the new age professes love and light, and seems to be effective in some ways - it is populated by unclean spirits, also known as demons. In the new age, they're referred to as "negative energy" or "entities," yet these are created beings with an evil agenda to lure souls away from Jesus.

Before I was saved, I loved to spend time in new age shops and believed they were filled with "positive energy." Yet, right after I was saved I got headaches being around new age items and practices. The

CHAPTER 1: NO FELLOWSHIP WITH DARKNESS

very beings (demons) who I mistakenly believed were angels throughout my life were counterfeiters.

You may struggle with wanting to keep certain new age items that hold sentimental value, or because it was expensive, or you just like the way that it looks. Perhaps someone gave you a new age item which you'll never use, yet you hesitate to throw it out because it was a gift. These are examples of where we need to turn to prayer for strength and discernment.

You may even become angry with me as you read this book and believe I'm being legalistic with my suggestions. *Legalism* is the false teaching that we're saved by our good works. Of course, we're saved by our faith in Jesus' work on the cross - and not our own works. Once we're saved, we're given a new heart and released from our former slavery to sin. As a result, we desire to please and obey God. Good works such as removing idols and other condemned items from your home, is *evidence* of salvation - not the *cause* of salvation.

Always ask:

- Does this glorify God?
- Is this a fleshly desire or rebelliousness?
- Am I trusting in the Lord instead of my own strength and will?

Remember what the Bible says about a little leaven spoiling everything in 1 Corinthians 5:6. There's no such thing as keeping an insignificant new age item, or thinking that one new age item won't matter. A small amount of sin can spread and affect many areas of your life, including having guilt or shame because deep down you know it's wrong.

This isn't legalism, because we're not saved by our good works of removing new age items. We're saved by God's grace and mercy, through our faith in Jesus. Then, when we're saved, we're given a new heart that wants to obey and please God. So, our obedience in removing these objects is a *fruit* or a result of salvation, and not the *root* or the cause of salvation.

Some may argue, "Well, we have freedom in Christ!" Yes, we do, yet but our freedom isn't a justification of sin and disobedience.

> *"For you were called to freedom, brothers. Only do not use your freedom as an opportunity for the flesh, but through love serve one another."* Galatians 5:13

Christian freedom isn't a license to sin; it's being free of the slavery to sin that we were once controlled by until God saved us out of darkness.

If we hang on to New Age tools, symbols, or teachings, we're essentially saying to God, "I trust You, but I still need this." God wants our whole heart, our undivided attention, and our full surrender.

The Bible is a lamp which shines light upon our path, so that we know which way to go. God's Word is clear that we as Christians should have nothing to do with new age items or practices:

> *"You cannot drink the cup of the Lord and the cup of demons. You cannot partake of the table of the Lord and the table of demons."* 1 Corinthians 10:21

New Age Objects Belonging to Someone Else

If the new age objects belong to someone in your home who isn't a Christian, or who doesn't agree to throw away the items, then you'll want to turn to prayer for wisdom and strength. Pray for the heart, conviction, and salvation of anyone in your home who's resistant to purging new age deception.

When my elderly and unsaved mother lived in my home, I threw away some of her blasphemous and heretical new age and Christian Science

CHAPTER 1: NO FELLOWSHIP WITH DARKNESS

new thought books without her permission. I prayed about it, and my desire to please and obey God exceeded my desire to temporarily please my mother. After all, true love is sharing the Gospel with the lost (which I did) and pointing them to the narrow path and away from darkness. I believe that I honored my mother by helping her to be away from dark influences.

You may have a different view of how to handle similar situations. Some possible solutions are to keep the new age items away from where you primarily stay in the house. Keep those items in the garage or in the other person's room, for example.

Prayerfully Walking Through Your Home

Each chapter has a checklist to use when walking through your home to remove the new age items. Pray for the Holy Spirit to lead you as you walk through your home. Be sure to also check in your closets, purses, coat pockets, drawers, garage, suitcases, attic, basement, storage shed, in your yard and on your patio and balcony. We found new age items in old forgotten moving boxes. Let this be a prayerful process of glorifying the Lord. Be sure to also look in your car and your office - anywhere that you spend time.

With each item, ask: "Is this glorifying to God?"

We don't want any items in our home that glorify paganism, the occult, new age, new thought, false teachings, or darkness.

Always, we want to turn to God for His support. Getting rid of new age items is an intense and possibly life-changing experience. Please don't let this be a fearful process, as we're not "demon slaying." We're prayerfully scouring our home for items which glorify darkness.

For me, the process happened in waves as I continued to find new age objects "hidden" in moving boxes, suitcases, and other areas of my home that I'd forgotten about. Each time that I discovered a new age item, I repeated the process of destroying it and throwing it away.

As you destroy and throw items away, it's always a good idea to repent for sins. We were forgiven through Jesus' shed blood upon the cross the moment that we believed the Gospel and turned to Him. Still, there are consequences for prior sins and we will continue to sin until we get to Heaven. Of course, as Christians our sins grieve us - unlike before we were saved when we were callous and rebellious toward God. We're called to repent whenever the Holy Spirit convicts us of a sin, so repenting is part of the process of getting new age items out of your home:

> *"If we confess our sins, he is faithful and just to forgive us our sins and to cleanse us from all unrighteousness."* 1 John 1:9

My prayer is that God will use this book to point people away from new age deception, and toward Jesus and Bible study. I also pray that this guidebook is helpful for you as you clear your home from deception.

All Glory to God, *Doreen*

Chapter 2: Reducing Spiritual Warfare in Your Home

Removing new age and occultic items from your home is also important because these items can be connected to spiritual warfare as this passage in Joshua 24:14-15 explains about the importance of rejecting idolatry:

> *"Now therefore fear the Lord and serve him in sincerity and in faithfulness. Put away the gods that your fathers served beyond the River and in Egypt and serve the Lord.*
>
> *And if it is evil in your eyes to serve the Lord, choose this day whom you will serve, whether the gods your fathers served in the region beyond the River, or the gods of the Amorites in whose land you dwell. But as for me and my house, we will serve the Lord."*

This verse from Deuteronomy 7:26 is also convicting about the destruction that accompanies having items in our home that are an abomination to the Lord:

> *"And you shall not bring an abominable thing into your house and become devoted to destruction like it."*

Having items in our home that are from practice and beliefs which the Bible condemns can bring the entire household under judgment. We see the obedience of the new Christians burning their expensive sorcery books and equipment in Acts 19:19. This is about obeying and trusting God.

When I was first saved, I suffered tremendously from spiritual warfare. There was a palpable demonic presence in my home that I'd never before experienced. It was so oppressive that I had insomnia. The demons who'd previously pretended to be my "guardian angels" were now punishing me because I was following Jesus instead of them.

As a new Christian dealing with spiritual warfare for the first time, I was initially influenced by the movie War Room, which portrayed the lead actress screaming at the devil to get out. So, I tried this because a deliverance minister insisted that "Jesus gave us authority to cast out demons." Yet, I found that screaming at the devil and commanding demons isn't wise or effective - even if we add the "in Jesus' name" tagline.

The Bible doesn't show believers commanding demons with loud declarations or having dramatic confrontations with the devil. It shows Jesus casting demons out of unsaved people, and the apostles quietly casting out demons. There are no instructions in the New Testament epistles to the church to conduct deliverance or cast out demons. Instead, God's Word instructs and equips us for dealing with spiritual warfare.

But I hadn't yet read the whole Bible, and I was desperate to get relief from the spiritual warfare. So, I turned to deliverance ministries. I also bought a book that guaranteed that if I said the prayers on its pages that it would "route out demons."

We also asked a local Pentecostal pastor to come to our home to help reduce spiritual warfare. He put drops of oil all over our home and yard. The pastor explained that this was "anointing oil" that would keep demons away from our home.

CHAPTER 2: REDUCING SPIRITUAL WARFARE IN YOUR HOME

Yet, despite all of these human efforts, the spiritual warfare in our home persisted and even seemed to increase. Why? Because those efforts weren't grounded in Scripture. They were based upon feelings and opinions.

Finally, I found relief through these measures that *are* Biblical:

1. **Praying.** The demons are afraid of Jesus, and we can pray for Him to cast out the demons. After all, Jesus is with believers always until the end of time. Why would we send a toddler like ourselves into battle, when we can pray for the King of Kings to cast out the demons? Besides, the demons are crafty and cunning and they take advantage of humans who try to have 1-on-1 conversations with them. It takes just as much time to pray for Jesus to cast out the demons as it does for us to try to do it on our own. New Age and the occult are do-it-yourself spiritual paths. So, it took awhile for my husband and I to adjust and learn how to trust in the Lord and to lean upon *His* strength instead of trying to do everything in our own strength.

2. **Getting new age and occult items out of our home.** My husband and I had many of the items that are described and listed in this book. We scoured our home to find and throw away every new age and occult item. We opened every box in our garage, looked through every closet and drawer, and even looked on our patio and in our yard to locate items from our new age past.

3. **Playing audios of the Bible daily, to saturate our minds with God's Word.** We especially do this as we're falling asleep at night since much of the spiritual warfare that I went through occurred at night. We listen to the free ESV Bible app that's available in the App Stores. It has an audio feature with an optional timer, which is perfect for when you're following asleep. Our favorite narrator on the app is David Cochran Heath.

4. **Following the Bible's exhortations and instructions for dealing with spiritual warfare:** submit to God, resist the devil, and he will flee (James 4:7); be sober-minded and alert (1 Peter 5:8); and to put on the Armor of God (Ephesians 6:10-18).
5. **Sincerely praising God.** Isaiah 61:3 KJV describes exchanging the spirit of heaviness for the garment of praise. Well, the spiritual warfare I was experiencing did feel like heaviness upon my body and soul. So, I got on my knees and praised God from my heart for all that I was grateful. The heaviness lifted, praise the Lord, and was one more blessing for which to praise God!

The Bible equips us for dealing with the inevitable spiritual warfare that all Christians experience. We're told to:

- have no fellowship with darkness (Ephesians 5:11)
- to not partner with lawlessness and have no fellowship with darkness (2 Corinthians 6:14-15)
- to have no idols or other abominations in our home (Deuteronomy 7:26)
- detroy any items of sorcery (Acts 19:19)

Sin gives the devil a foothold in our lives (Ephesians 4:26-27) and breaks our fellowship with God (Isaiah 59:2). Obedience, such as removing new age and occultic items from your home restores fellowship with God (1 John 1:7).

Listen to these powerful warnings about not having pagan items in your home:

Joshua 7:11-13 says, "You will not be able to stand against your enemies until you remove what is set apart" when forbidden items caused God's protection to lift from the people.

Deuteronomy 7:25-26 commands to not bring an abomination into

CHAPTER 2: REDUCING SPIRITUAL WARFARE IN YOUR HOME

your home, "and thereby become designated for destruction like it; you shall utterly detest it, for it is designated for destruction."

Cleaning Your House as the Bible Instructs

The enemy is cunning. and he tries to tempt Christians to overly focus upon demons and spiritual warfare in unbiblical ways - using rituals and objects, and not relying upon Jesus.

Even "Christianized" versions of spiritual warfare can become idolatrous. When we trust in annointing oil, or grape juice, or shofar horns, or decreeing and declaring instead of God's mighty power, we're essential trying to replace God's power with symbolic human control.

We are called to:

- Submit to God
- Resist the devil (James 4:7)
- Stand firm in faith and truth
- Walk in obedience and holiness

So, let's begin this journey of obediently cleaning your home of any object which represents disobedience to God. Let's remove the objects from your home that are amongst the sins for which Jesus our Lord and Savior died on the cross. We'll start with removing idolatrous statues, as the next chapter explains.

Chapter 3: New Age and Idolatrous Statues & Artwork to Remove from Your Home

When I was first saved, I didn't fully understand what idolatry was. I thought idols were only golden calves or ancient pagan totems. But as I studied the Bible more deeply, I realized how subtle and widespread idolatry can be - and that includes within our homes.

Many of us have unknowingly allowed objects into our lives that conflict with God's commandments. An idol is anything that's on the throne of our heart, instead of Jesus who rightly belongs there. Idols can distract us from Jesus and the Gospel, and idols can never bring us fulfillment, peace, or salvation.

As you know, the Bible is filled with warnings against idolatry, especially the first and second commandments which are still for today:

> *"You shall have no other gods before me. You shall not make for yourself a carved image, or any likeness of anything that is in heaven above, or that is in the earth beneath, or that is in the water under the earth. You shall not bow down to them or serve them, for I the Lord your God am a jealous God, visiting the inequity of the fathers on the children to the third and fourth generation of those who hate me, but showing steadfast love to thousands of those who love me and keep my commandments." Exodus 20:3-6*

CHAPTER 3: NEW AGE AND IDOLATROUS STATUES & ARTWORK TO...

The Old Testament describes how pagan worship statues are abominations to God, and that the statues can't hear or answer prayers so the pagan worship practices are futile (c.f., Psalm 135:15-18).
The New Testament also warns about idolatry:

> "Therefore, my beloved, flee from idolatry." 1 Corinthians 10:14
> "Little children, keep yourselves from idols." 1 John 5:21

Idolatry is listed as a work of the flesh, in contrast to the list of the fruit of Spirit in Galatians 5. Idolaters won't be allowed into the New Heaven, but will be cast into the lake of fire for eternity (Revelation 21:8,22:15). So, this is a very serious and potentially salvific (difference between Heaven and hell) issue.

The most classic form of idolatry are statues, so let's begin there. After all, the golden calf was a statue.

Statues of Other Religions or Deities

Many homes contain statues like:

- Buddha figures (often for "peace" or "luck")
- Goddess statues such as Quan Yin
- Hindu deities (like Ganesh, Lakshmi, Kali, or Shiva)
- Egyptian symbols, like Isis wings or the Eye of Horus
- Statues from other cultures and religions

These statues may be used as décor, yet they're not harmless. Even if you're not actively "worshiping" them, they still represent false gods and spiritual systems that oppose the gospel.

There's also the danger of someone seeing the statue when visiting your home and then falsely believing that Christians can have pagan or false gospel statues. That's the definition of causing someone to stumble that the Bible warns about:

> *"But take care that this right of yours does not somehow become a stumbling block to the weak."* 1 Corinthians 8:9

I started acquiring Hindu and Buddhist statues after becoming fascinated by the statues at the yoga studio I attended. Most yoga studios have statues of the Hindu deity Shiva and also the Buddhist goddess Quan Yin. At first, I bought the statues because I liked the way they looked. Yet, I soon began praying to them and lighting candles at their feet. Sometimes, I'd even give the statues an "offering" of freshly cut flowers from my garden.

Before I was saved, I had a large statue of a Tibetan Buddhist monk in my home. I gold-leafed the statue, and found myself "talking" to him. Thereafter, I started praying to him (I've repented and no longer do this).

Perhaps you don't pray to your statues like I did. However, do these statues glorify God? Could they cause a visitor to your home, or your children, to stumble into idolatry?

> *"You shall not make for yourself a carved image . . . You shall not bow down to them or serve them, for I the Lord your God am a jealous God . . ."* Exodus 20:4-5

I also had a statue of a Chinese warrior in my home. He wasn't a spiritual or religious deity, yet he did represent war. I'd purchased the statue because I thought it looked cool, and probably because I thought it was an item for protection. Yet, as soon as I was saved, that warrior statue went into the dumpster.

We don't donate or resell these statues. We destroy them. We smash the idols. We get them out of our homes. Remember Acts 19:19 - when new believers burned their occult items publicly? It wasn't wasteful. It was worshipful.

"Christian" Statues

In addition to statues of pagan deities, Christian-themed statues and artwork can also be idols. I believe there's some Christian liberty in this area, so you'll need to pray for the Holy Spirit's leading. If your conscience tells you not to have these statues, we must follow our conscience.

I had a Mother Mary statue that I directed prayers and worship toward. Although I wasn't raised Roman Catholic, the new age incorporates their beliefs about praying to (or "venerating") saints and archangels as intercessors for prayer. When we'd travel, my husband and I always visited Roman Catholic cathedrals and lit candles at the feet of statues.

It took Bible study for us to break this habit, and to remember that God's Word says that Jesus is the only mediator between humanity and Father God (1 Timothy 2:5) and that deceased humans can't hear or answer our prayers (Ecclesiastes 9:5). So, her statue went into the home.

In addition, I had a bronze statue representing Jesus that stood near my front door. I believed the statue would somehow protect our home. Yet, the Bible doesn't describe what Jesus looked like so the statue was a vague representation. I found myself saying, "Hello Jesus" when I'd see the statue, which is a third commandment violation of using the Lord's name in vain. Some theologians believe that having statues or paintings that represent Jesus is a second commandment violation against no graven images, especially if you're worshiping or praying to the statue.

You might have in your home:

- Angel figurines
- Statues of Jesus
- Figurines of Roman Catholic saints, such as Mother Mary or Saint Francis
- Icon images on candles or artwork
- Wall art with scenes representing Jesus or the angels.

These items can violate the Second Commandment:

> *"You shall not make for yourself a carved image, or any likeness of anything that is in heaven above . . . You shall not bow down to them or serve them . . ."* Exodus 20:4-5

We must ask: Am I honoring God with this item, or am I replacing my worship of Him with a visual image? If the statue is causing you to focus more on the image itself than on God, it might be time to reevaluate its place in your home.

Statues of Jesus, Mary, or Roman Catholic saints can unintentionally plant false images in our minds. The Bible only hints at what Jesus looked like, and doesn't describe His physical appearance. Isaiah 53:2 prophetically characterized the Messiah as average looking, with no extraordinary physical features to make Him stand out during His earthly ministry. Perhaps that's why Judas had to point out Jesus during his betrayal at Gethsemane, since Jesus didn't stand out in a crowd.

So, statues could give us a visual image that distracts us when we're reading the Bible and imagining the artist's rendering. Every part of the Bible is God-breathed (2 Timothy 3:16), and that includes what God didn't put into the Bible. God intentionally left out what we don't need to know, such as Jesus' physical appearance.

Statues of deceased Roman Catholic saints can veer into necromancy or mediumship, if we're using the statues as a vehicle to pray to or talk to them. The Bible commands us not to engage in communication with the dead, because God is protecting us from demons masquerading as saints or deceased loved ones.

Deceased people can't hear prayers or conversations from the living (c.f., Ecclesiastes 9:5). So not only do prayers, venerations, intercession requests, or conversations with saints violate God's commandments but they're also ineffective since the saints can't hear us.

"For there is one God, and there is one mediator between God and men, the man Christ Jesus." 1 Timothy 2:5

Jesus is our only mediator between humanity and our Heavenly Father God. We don't need, nor should we utilize, a statue as an intermediary or as a means for requesting intercession for prayers.

Whether or not a statue of Jesus violates the Second Commandment (2CV) is a debate in different denominations. I personally believe that they are a 2CV from my prayers, studies, and conscience.

Those who believe that Jesus statues are a 2CV, approach Nativity scene statuary in one of these ways:

- An empty manger to represent the anticipation of Jesus' birth.
- Symbolic representation of baby Jesus such as a candle or lantern, as He is the light of the world.
- Parchment paper scroll with Scripture about Jesus' birth, placed in the manger.
- A statue that doesn't portray details of the baby's face.

Again, I think there's some Christian liberty with statutes of Jesus and other Biblical figures. If you can honestly say to yourself and the Holy

Spirit that your statues aren't used for any form of prayer, intercession requests, or worship - and if your conscience is fine with having them - I believe they could have a place in a Christian home. Or if the statue is a family heirloom and nobody uses the statue for worship, it makes sense to keep it.

Same with angel statues. Of course, we must remember that the Bible's descriptions of what angels and cherubim look like is very different than modern angel statues. Most people wouldn't want a statue of a being with multiple eyes, heads, wheels, and wings in their home - yet that's how the Bible describes angels.

The Bible is crystal-clear that we are not to pray to angels, nor try to invoke them (Colossians 2:18; Revelation 19:10). Scripture also warns us that the devil pretends to be an angel in order to deceive us (2 Corinthians 11:14).

I personally can't have angel statues anymore because they remind me of my days as a blasphemous heretic before God saved me. My conscience wouldn't allow me to have any statues of Biblical figurines, and certainly not pagan statues.

We don't need images, statues, or intermediaries. Jesus' sacrifice on our behalf tore the veil, and we have direct access to the Father through Him.

Garden or Backyard Statues

Your home also includes your outdoor space. Whether it's a backyard, front lawn, balcony, weathervane, roof top garden, fountain, swimming pool mural, or on your patio, it's important that statues or other decorations glorify God and not glorify darkness.

Some common new age items that professing Christians may have in their outdoor space without realizing the new age significance includes:

CHAPTER 3: NEW AGE AND IDOLATROUS STATUES & ARTWORK TO...

- **Green Man statues.** They're usually flat and embossed with eyes peaking through oak leaves. Green Man is believed to be an actual nature deity in New Age teachings.
- **Polytheistic garden statues.** Some people believe that Buddha statues give an air of tranquility in a garden, yet it's pointing away from Jesus as the only One who can save our souls (John 14:6) and it could cause someone to stumble into polytheism if they see a deity statue in the yard of a professing Christian.
- **Garden Gnomes.** I realize that some people think that they're cute and that the professing Christian store, Hobby Lobby, sells them. But when you've been in the darkness of new age, you realize that there's actual demons who masquerade as gnomes, menehunes, and other elemental spirits.
- **Fairy Statues.** My mom gave me a gift of a terra cotta fairy statue for my backyard garden when I lived in Dana Point, California. I had a fascination with fairies ever since childhood when my mom bought me a book of fairy tale stories that had a painting of fairies on the cover. Within months of getting this fairy statue, I was soon imagining that I was talking with fairies and I even wrote a book on the topic. Just like demons can masquerade as angels (2 Corinthians 11:14), so too can they masquerade as elemental spirits.
- **Fairy gardens and Fairy doors.** While these decorations can seem innocent and whimsical, I can tell you from personal experience that they can be a part of spiritual warfare and oppression. Be very cautious with these items! They can lead to altered states of trances and even imagining that the fairies are with you. Fairy doors placed upon your trees is an invitation for demons to arrive. I personally wouldn't have these items in my home or garden.
- **Dragon statues.** Even when I was in the new age, I was wary of dragons. Just like the other elemental spirits, demons can masquerade as a dragon for those who believe they can connect

with dragon spirits. This is similar to the new age and shamanic beliefs in "power animals" or "spirit animals."

- **Garden crystals.** Some people have large amethyst geodes in their backyards. If these are simply there for beauty and to appreciate God's creation, then there' no problem. It's an issue if the crystals are viewed as idols that have magical mystical powers on their own, or if the crystals are used for divination.
- **Labyrinths** used for mystical walking meditations that lead to altered states of consciousness. This type of walking meditation is connected to Greek mythology and indigenous traditions, and often includes instructions for breathwork which can lead to trances. The Bible never instructs us to engage in physical rituals, breathwork, or emptying our minds to draw near to God or to gain wisdom. Instead, we are to turn to Scripture and prayers for God's wisdom.
- **Wind Chimes** decorated with New Age symbols or small statues. Wind chimes are spiritually neutral, so they're not a problem unless they have New Age symbolism on them or have a pagan statue as part of the design, or if the sound leads to altered states of consciousness and trances.

CHAPTER 3: NEW AGE AND IDOLATROUS STATUES & ARTWORK TO...

"Christian" Wall Art

The art in your home could also be an idol. The Holy Spirit can shed light upon whether images in your home promote idolatry or violate the Second Commandment.

When I was first saved and had thrown away and destroyed my pagan statues and paintings, I replaced them with wall art depicting Jesus. But then I noticed that I was reflexively saying, "Hello Lord" or "Hello Jesus" whenever I'd walk by these paintings. I even knelt in prayer before one of my Jesus paintings.

Upon prayerful reflection, I realized that I viewed these paintings as a window to reach the real Jesus. I knew the paintings were symbols, yet they were idols because I believed they were tools of worship so that my prayers were heard. As a result of this conviction, I threw away my paintings that represented Jesus. I admit that it was a painful process, yet it was necessary to avoid idolatry of the paintings.

We don't need any physical tools to have our prayers heard. The Bible says that God hears the prayer of the righteous when the prayers are aligned with God's will. So, prayer is about our heart, mind, and action being submitted to God's will.

New Age Wall Art

New Age wall art doesn't belong in a Christian home, since it could lead to pagan practices. For example, new age slogans teach false works-based beliefs like:

- Believe in yourself
- Follow your heart

These slogans contradict the Bible's teachings to trust in the Lord and not our heart or our own understanding. As someone who followed her heart for decades before God saved me, I can attest that it's a destructive way to live. We need to instead study the Bible daily and pray for God's wisdom to lead us.

New Age paintings can also be symbols, such as:

- The Hindu Ohm symbol, which is often displayed in yoga studios
- Horus' eye in a triangle, which is a pagan and occultic symbol
- Ouija board wall hangings
- Chakras or manadala images of shapes in concentric circles
- Lotus flower images *can* be a symbol of yoga or new age meditation

CHAPTER 3: NEW AGE AND IDOLATROUS STATUES & ARTWORK TO...

- The phases of the moon symbols used in Wicca and for witchcraft

New Age wall art can also include paintings of pagan deities. Before I was saved, I had images of Hindu and Buddhist goddesses on my walls, because I believed that these images could help me in my life. After God saved me, I destroyed the paintings and tossed them into the dumpster.

New Age wall art commonly displays elemental beings such as fairies, mermaids, and unicorns. My concern with these images is that they can lead to altered state of conscious trances, especially in children who look at the paintings. We also know that demons can masquerade as these elemental beings, in order to deceive people about "magical powers." So, I personally don't believe Christian homes should have these images.

Every October, stores sell Halloween decorations that glorify darkness. We need to be discerning and prayerfully consider whether these items belong in your Christian home. For example, stores sell Ouija board divination wall hangings at Halloween time. Why would we want to decorate our home with anything that glorifies a sin for which Jesus died?

Halloween decorations that glorify death such as headstones, skeletons, and ghosts aren't appropriate for Christian homes - no matter how normal or whimsical they seem. We're exhorted as Christians to glorify God in *everything* that we do. There's no exception to that exhortation for Halloween.

Along the same line, some wall art glorifies violence. This includes wall art portraying violent or immodest illustrations of superheroes or video game characters, marketed to children. We have Christian liberty, yet we also need to pray for and obey the Holy Spirit's lead.

Some professing Christians argue: "Well, God knows my heart!" as if that's a ticket to justify rebelling against God's commandments. God *does* know our heart, and He knows when we're steeped in willfulness rather than submitting to Him.

Wall art that glorifies anything other than God needs to be removed. The new age appropriates from other culture's spirituality and religious practices, and then uses them as props and decorations.

For example, "dream catchers" are part of Native American spirituality about catching bad dreams with the spider web of the dream catcher. So, how is catching bad dreams in a spider web glorifying to God? I interviewed a Mayan man who was a shaman, until God saved him and he's now a Christian. This man told me that even though dream catchers are part of his native culture, he wouldn't have one now as a Christian.

I've sadly seen dream catchers for sale at the professing Christian store, Hobby Lobby. Dream catchers aren't Christian and they don't belong in any Christian home or store. In addition, having this item in your home could cause a visitor or a child in the home to stumble into Native American spirituality. Dream catchers would be an item for Christians to discard out of their homes.

Masks as wall art also need to be addressed. If they're masks of war, or used in paganism, we must question why we would want them in our homes. If you have any masks from other cultures hanging as wall art, pray for the Holy Spirit's guidance about whether or not this item glorifies God and belongs in your Christian home. If the Holy Spirit convicts you to get rid of the item, please listen to His guidance.

Icon Prayer or Votive Candles

In the new age, we used tall slender glass candles for protection and "manifesting." Each candle had an image representing a Biblical figure, such as Jesus, Mary, or Archangel Michael. We lit these candles and prayed that they would keep us safe.

These candles are primarily used in Roman Catholic, Anglican, and

Orthodox churches. They're sometimes called "seven-day candles" because they're designed to burn continuously for a week to symbolize ongoing prayer.

As Christians who've studied the Bible, we know that God doesn't require us to light a candle in order for our prayers to be heard. We also know that deceased people, such as Roman Catholic saints, can't hear our prayers, venerations, requests for intercession, or other conversations (Ecclesiastes 9:5). Jesus is the *only* mediator between humanity and God the Father (1 Timothy 2:5), not Roman Catholic saints.

We also know from Biblical descriptions of Archangel Michael, that he's not a personal guardian angel who responds to our prayers for protection or other favors. We need to be careful, since the Bible says that the devil can masquerade as an angel of light pretending to be Archangel Michael. That certainly happened to me.

These candles aren't new age, yet they're not Biblical either. If the candles are idols to you, or objects that cause you to stumble into idolatry, necromancy or mediumship (talking to the dead), it's best to get them out of your home.

Pray for Strength and Wisdom

If you're reluctant to toss any artwork, take your prayers to the Lord for discernment, conviction, and strength. I realize that we get attached to items, and there may also be a reluctance to throw away expensive items.

My strong advice is to walk through each room while praying for the Holy Spirit to lead your actions. The Holy Spirit will nudge you to throw away items that are idols or that could cause you or others to stumble. If the item isn't glorifying God or is distracting you from the Gospel, it's time to let the item go.

You may notice items that have been there for years and that you've forgotten about. Sometimes we become blind or habituated to what's on our walls. We walk past it so many times that we stop noticing. That's why it's important to pray for discernment, strength, and wisdom.

It might seem extreme to throw out an expensive statue or discard a painting you once loved. But remember - obeying God your Creator and the One who saved you is worth it. Your home is a place of worship. Every object should either glorify God, or at least not distract you from Him.

> *"Do not be unequally yoked with unbelievers. For what partnership has righteousness with lawlessness? Or what fellowship has light with darkness?"* 2 Corinthians 6:14

As we grow in Christ, we want to remove every trace of the spiritual confusion and deception we once walked in. We don't need reminders of the New Age in our surroundings. We need reminders of truth.

And once again: please don't pass these items on to someone else. Don't sell or donate them. Destroy or discard them.

Removing Idolatrous Statues and Artwork

In each of the chapters that lists categories of what to remove, you'll find a checklist that may be helpful in this process. Here are some practical steps as you use this checklist:

1. **Pray first.** As you walk through your home carrying a trash can or trash bag, ask the Holy Spirit to reveal what needs to go.
2. **Walk through each room slowly.** Let God guide you.
3. **Physically destroy the items if possible.** Crush, break, burn, or

CHAPTER 3: NEW AGE AND IDOLATROUS STATUES & ARTWORK TO...

pour water on them. (Just like Acts 19:19.) In some cases, you'll bag them first and destroy them second.
4. **Bag them and discard them.** Don't hesitate. Don't second-guess.
5. **Get the bags of garbage out of your home and away from your home as soon as possible.**

Many have shared that removing these items was like lifting a spiritual fog and they noticed a reduction in spiritual warfare as we discussed in Chapter 2.

"Whether you eat or drink, or whatever you do, do all to the glory of God." 1 Corinthians 10:31

The bottom line is: Whatever you do, do it for God's glory.

Checklist for Finding and Removing Idolatrous Statues and Artwork from Your Home

On the next page you'll see a checklist of rooms to use if you'd like, as you go through your home to find and remove idolatrous statues and artwork. Please remember to check your outdoor spaces, your garage, your attic and basement, storage shed, and your basement.

CHECKLIST FOR FINDING AND REMOVING IDOLATROUS STATUES AND...

KITCHEN	LIVING ROOM
☐	☐
☐	☐
☐	☐
☐	☐
☐	☐
☐	☐
☐	☐

HALLWAY / ENTRY	BEDROOM
☐	☐
☐	☐
☐	☐
☐	☐
☐	☐
☐	☐
☐	☐

OTHER	BATHROOM
☐	☐
☐	☐
☐	☐
☐	☐
☐	☐
☐	☐
☐	☐

Chapter 4: New Age Divination Tools to Remove from Your Home

When I began clearing New Age items from my home, divination tools were one of the first things to go. These items had been my daily companions - tools I used to try to understand life, control outcomes, or receive guidance. Then God used Scripture to open my eyes to what I was really doing: stepping outside of God's will and trusting in deceptive, spiritual counterfeits.

Let's look at the main categories of divination tools and why they have no place in a Christian home.

Oracle and Divination Cards

Whether they're called "angel cards," "power animal cards," "goddess cards," "tarot," "oracle cards" or "divination cards," these tools all serve the same purpose: to reveal hidden knowledge and gain insight outside of God's Word.

The promise of secret hidden knowledge was how the serpent lured Eve into sinning. The devil has been making the same promise ever since.

The cards seem to be a shortcut way to receive inside information from the spirit world. At least that's what I used to believe. Now I realize that cards are vague, and we impose our own wishes and agenda

CHAPTER 4: NEW AGE DIVINATION TOOLS TO REMOVE FROM YOUR HOME

in interpreting them. The demons also intervene into card readings, to point people away from the only One who can save souls: Jesus.

Before I was saved, I was involved in publishing "angel cards" and "goddess cards" which are based upon the tarot system. Some people still sell used and illegally printed bootleg copies and also non-English copies of my old cards. If they had been self-published, I would've pulled the cards and my old books off the market the minute I was saved in 2017. Unfortunately, the cards were licensed to 38 foreign publishers and some are even publishing the cards illegally without permission. So, the best that I can do is to pray that people don't sell, buy, or use cards . . . and that if they do have cards, that they destroy them and throw them away.

The Bible is clear in the Old and New Testament that we are *not* to practice divination. God exhorts us to trust Him, not divination tools.

> *"There shall not be found among you anyone who . . . practices divination or tells fortunes or interprets omens."* Deuteronomy 18:10 (truncated)

These practices are clearly forbidden - not because God wants to restrict us, but because He wants to protect us. When we use cards to receive "guidance," we're attempting to bypass prayer and Scripture. Even worse, these cards can be an entry point to deception since demonic spirits masquerade as "guides" or "angels of light" (2 Corinthians 11:14).

God doesn't contradict Himself, so He doesn't communicate through tools of divination. Neither do God's angels. God speaks through His Word, and through biblical counsel. The cards aren't from Him - even if they use Biblical-sounding words like "God," "light," or "angels."

If you have any divination cards, it's time to throw them out. Burn them if you can, or pour water or oil on them, or shred them so that they're unusable in case another person finds them.

"Affirmation cards" can also be idols if they cause you to look to yourself for wisdom, instead of to God. These cards have new age slogans about trusting your heart, following your dreams, believing in yourself, and so forth. While those may sounds like positive or normal sayings, they can be the devil's subtle way of putting yourself upon the throne of your heart. It's self-idolatry, which leads to dangerous pridefulness.

The small cards called "angel cards" can also be idolatrous and a divination tool, so it's best to discard them. Same with the cards about Jesus that I made before I was saved. Be very discerning and listen to the Holy Spirit about any cards - even the so-called "Christian cards." It's best to avoid them or throw them out. The only exception that I can think of would be educational flash cards used for memorizing Scripture or to learn Biblical languages such as Koine Greek or Hebrew.

Pendulums

A pendulum is often a crystal or weighted object attached to a chain, used to receive "yes" or "no" answers by the direction that it swings on the chain. Pendulums are another form of divination that are forbidden by God.

God created the beautiful crystals that hang from pendulum chains, and there are crystals in the Bible. However, the Bible never says we're to use God's creations such as crystals for divination. Some speculate that the Bible's mentions of casting lots or the Urim and Thummim were crystals, yet the Bible doesn't say that. There are *no* descriptions of either method, perhaps to prevent us from mimicking those practices which were God-controlled and which ceased long ago.

Using a pendulum places your trust in an object, not in God. I also believe that the movement of the pendulum is affected by the intentions of the person holding it. *Should I quit my job? Oh, look! The pendulum*

CHAPTER 4: NEW AGE DIVINATION TOOLS TO REMOVE FROM YOUR HOME

is saying yes! Divination is part self-fulfilling prophecy and wishful thinking, and part demonic influence. Either way, these pendulums don't belong in Christians' lives or their homes.

"Trust in the Lord with all your heart, and do not lean on your own understanding. In all your ways acknowledge Him, and He will make straight your paths." Proverbs 3:5-6

If you've used a pendulum, ask the Lord to forgive you. Then destroy it - don't pass it on to other people. Some pendulums have metal points instead of crystal points, yet they're just as much condemned as divination tools. Just as with divination cards, these tools are often subtle invitations into darker deception.

Rune Stones

These small stones or pieces of wood are inscribed with symbols from an ancient Norse alphabet called "rune script." Each rune symbol is believed to have a mystical meaning and power. Rune stones are a divination tool to try to gain guidance and secret hidden knowledge. The stones are laid out in patterns, and then interpreted like a tarot reader giving an interpretation.

Divination is a condemned practice, no matter what the tool used for divination. The mythological basis of rune stones is steeped in Norse polytheism. Rune stones aren't appropriate for Christians and should be removed from the home in a way that other people can't find them and risk being deceived by them either.

Ouija Board

Also known as a "spirit board," the Ouija is a flat board printed with alphabetical letters, numbers, and the words "yes," "no," and "goodbye." Uses place their fingers upon a pointer called a "planchette" and ask questions of the spirit world. Some people use the Ouija board to try to contact deceased loved ones in the condemned practice of mediumship, and others use the board to contact any spirit that wishes to communicate. Either way, these are spiritually dangerous practices. Demons use Ouija boards to deliver deceptive messages to people, and to tempt them into further occultic practices. These demons definitely fail the "test of the spirits" in 1 John 4:1 as they never point people to the true Jesus.

Ouija boards, including any representation of a Ouija board such as wall art or jewelry, should be destroyed and removed from a Christian's home as soon as possible.

The I Ching or Chinese Fortune Sticks

The I Ching is an ancient Chinese divination tool, in which the user asks a question, then tosses coins or sticks to form a hexagram pattern. This pattern is then matched to written material which interprets this pattern and gives the person spiritual guidance.

Similarly, Chinese Fortune Sticks also called "oracle sticks" or "prophecy sticks," consist of long sticks in a cardboard tube. Each stick has a number or letter carved into it. The person asking the question shakes the container until a stick would fall out. The number on the stick was interpreted by a manuscript, to supposedly give the person an answer or a "fortune."

My paternal grandmother had this tool and my brother and I played with giving ourselves and each other "readings" with the sticks whenever we'd visit her. Even though she was a church-going and Bible-believing Presbyterian, she had this divination tool which influenced me to believe that it was fine for people to consult pagan systems like

CHAPTER 4: NEW AGE DIVINATION TOOLS TO REMOVE FROM YOUR HOME

this. So, we must remove divination items from our home because God condemns them and also because they can cause someone to stumble into paganism who visits our home.

Crystals

Let me be clear: crystals in and of themselves are spiritually neutral. God created them, and they're referenced throughout the Bible from Genesis to Revelation. However, the issue isn't the crystal - it's *how* we use it.

In the New Age, crystals are commonly believed to hold mystical energetic properties. New Agers believe that the color of the crystal determines whether it's to be used for protection, attracting love, increasing psychic abilities, healing, and so forth. Crystals are used in new age rituals and also placed into patterns on the floor called "grids." Each grid pattern and the specific crystals in the grid are supposed to help with various issues.

These practices are the condemned practice of *idolatry*, because they're based upon the belief that crystals have inherent magical powers apart from God. They put faith in the crystal, and not in God. This upside-down viewpoint is condemned in Romans 1:26 as "serving the creation instead of the Creator." It's similar to those who worship the stars and the moon, instead of God the creator of the stars and the moon.

Crystals are also used in making statues such as Hindu deities and Platonic geometric shapes. These crystal statues aren't neutral - they're designed for new age purposes, so they would absolutely be idols to remove from your Christian home.

Some people use crystals for the condemned practice of divination. For example, they will fill a bowl or velvet bag with crystals. Then, they or their client will close their eyes and select a crystal. There are various and conflicting new age systems which supposedly tell the meaning depending upon which crystal they select. It's very subjective like dream interpretation, and no one can agree on the meaning of each crystal.

Before I was saved, I used crystals to prepare me to give psychic readings by holding a clear quartz point between my two physical eyes to supposedly open my "third eye chakra" so I could have clairvoyant visions. I also wore purple crystal necklace pendants, especially sugalite and amethyst because I believed that the stones helped my psychic readings and channeling. I was practicing both idolatry and divination - a double-whammy of condemned practices. Praise God for saving me out of that delusional darkness!

I also want to ask my sisters in Christ to please refrain from calling it a "God wink" when you find a heart-shaped stone out in nature. That's a form of omen-interpreting which is condemned in Deuteronomy 18:10-12. We violate the Third Commandment when we ascribe something to God that's not from Him. Yes, God made the rock and shaped it. But it's not a personal wink to you.

Let's instead say, "Seeing this heart-shaped stone fills my heart with joy." It's not a wink from God confirming that you're on the right path, or so forth. So, if you have a collection of heart-shaped stones that could cause you to stumble into omen interpreting, please pray about whether it's time to return those stones somewhere outdoors away from your home.

New agers also engage in rituals to clear their crystals from "negative energy," such as placing the crystal outside during the full moon. Then, they have rituals to "charge" or "program" the crystal, which means they're instructing the crystal to perform specific tasks - which is more new age nonsense.

If you're placing your trust in a crystal instead of in God, it has become an idol. If you believe a stone can heal, cleanse, protect, or attract blessings, you're crediting God's creation instead of the Creator. All glory needs to go to God, and not His creations.

Now, if you simply appreciate a crystal's natural beauty, like you would a flower or a seashell, and you don't ascribe any power or energy to it, then it may be fine to keep. This is something to prayerfully discern with the Lord.

If your conscience is unsettled when you think about crystals, if it tempts you to relapse into the New Age, it's best to let them go. Since crystals are natural, you could throw them into a body of water such as a lake, river, or the ocean. Or you could bury the crystals away from your home, where they don't provide a temptation. I threw away my crystals in the dumpster. I've also discipled a few ladies who decided to put their crystal into a bag and smash them with a hammer.

Astrology Charts

God created the stars and the planets, yet His creations aren't to be used for divination. Astrology and horoscopes are forms of divination, because they're attempts to peak into the future as a way of predicting and controlling the future, instead of trusting our sovereign God.

Some argue that the Magi were astrologers, so therefore the Bible approves of astrology. First, there's nothing in the Bible that says that the Magi were astrologers. They were either magicians or wise men who followed the prophesied star to meet Jesus. Second, the Bible clearly condemns astrology as being an object of God's wrath (Isaiah 47:13-14) and an ineffective way to gain wisdom (Daniel 2:1-13).

We will discuss getting rid of astrology books and apps in other chapters. For now, let's see if you have any physical astrology charts in your home. Perhaps someone printed out your natal chart and gave it to you. This chart would be a drawing of a large circle showing the positions of the sun, moon, and various planets according to when and where you were born.

Usually, this drawing is accompanied by typed pages which seek to explain what your rising sign and the planetary positions mean about your personality. People often store these charts in a large envelope or folder, so it could be amongst your papers.

If you have an astrological chart in your home - even if it was a gift from a beloved person who meant well - please remove it from your home. It doesn't belong in a Christian home.

Other Divination Tools

The devil isn't creative, yet he's a crafty counterfeiter. So he invents many ways to deceive humans with various divination tools. Anything can be used for divination, if there's a belief that the object can yield special meaning, a personal private revelation, insightful guidance, or hidden secret knowledge.

As you go through the rooms in your home, prayerfully ask the Holy Spirit to guide you to find and remove anything that you may have used in the past for divination.

No Need for Divination Tools

People turn to divination to receive guidance and direction, yet any advice that's apart from God can't be trusted. You don't need cards, pendulums, sticks, stones, or crystals to make decisions or to receive guidance. Prayer, Bible study, and consulting with mature Christians who know the Bible are ways to get answers:

> *"Your word is a lamp to my feet and a light to my path." Psalm 119:105*

CHAPTER 4: NEW AGE DIVINATION TOOLS TO REMOVE FROM YOUR HOME

"If any of you lacks wisdom, let him ask God, who gives generously to all without reproach, and it will be given him." James 1:5

Checklist for Finding and Removing New Age Divination Tools from Your Home

Here's a checklist on the next page if you'd like to use this while going through your home to find and remove new age divination tools. Be sure to check your garage, attic, basement, closets, and outdoor spaces too.

CHECKLIST FOR FINDING AND REMOVING NEW AGE DIVINATION TOOLS...

KITCHEN	LIVING ROOM
☐	☐
☐	☐
☐	☐
☐	☐
☐	☐
☐	☐
☐	☐

HALLWAY / ENTRY	BEDROOM
☐	☐
☐	☐
☐	☐
☐	☐
☐	☐
☐	☐
☐	☐

OTHER	BATHROOM
☐	☐
☐	☐
☐	☐
☐	☐
☐	☐
☐	☐
☐	☐

Chapter 5: New Age Jewelry to Remove from Your Home

As Christians, our bodies are temples of the Holy Spirit (1 Corinthians 6:19). The jewelry and clothing that we wear can be glorifying to God, or glorifying to darkness in the case of new age jewelry and clothing. If someone sees a professing Christian wearing new age jewelry, it could influence that person to believe that it's okay for Christians to be involved with new age and paganism, when it's not.

With jewelry we have a lot of freedom in Christ; however, we have 3 considerations:

1. We shouldn't cause someone else to stumble by wearing jewelry that points to New Age or occult deception.

2. We shouldn't defy our conscience or the Holy Spirit's convictions.

3. We are to glorify God in everything we do, so if the jewelry is glorifying a false deity, that would not be glorifying God.

In this chapter, we'll look at new age jewelry. Then in Chapter 6, we'll examine new age clothing that needs to go in the dumpster or fire pit.

Jewelry with New Age Symbols

Sometimes, jewelry looks cute or even trendy, but the symbols tell a different story. Remember that those in the jewelry industry may be

CHAPTER 5: NEW AGE JEWELRY TO REMOVE FROM YOUR HOME

trying to "evangelize" their paganism through their jewelry. Some common new age symbols to beware of that commonly appear on necklace pendants, rings, and bracelet charms include:

- **Ohm symbol also known as Om or Ahm.** This is a Hindu Sanskrit letter that blasphemously glorifies the universe and a universal energy, instead of our Creator who made the universe. This symbol is widely used in yoga practices, since yoga is a Hindu worship practice of pagan deities.
- **Pentagrams, inverted stars, or inverted crosses.** These symbols rebelliously mock Christianity and promote Wiccan, witchcraft, occultic, or satanic rituals.
- **Chakra or "sacred geometry" pendants such as Metatron's cube.** These geometric shapes are used for new age healing and meditation methods, including yoga. Chakra symbols originated in Hinduism, and are commonly used in yoga classes.
- **The Eye of Horus, Isis Wings, or the "All-Seeing Eye."** Egyptian and Masonic symbolism often linked to secret societies or occultic practices.
- **Evil Eye; Hamsa hand.** Four concentric circles, with a small black circle in the middle representing an eye's pupil, surrounded by a light blue circle representing the eye's iris, then a white circle and a royal blue circle. The "evil eye" is often made of glass as a pendant or bracelet bead or charm. In Islamic and Hindu traditions, the "evil eye" is used for protection and to ward off "bad luck." Make sure also that you don't have this symbol as a decoration or "protection device" in your home. The Hamsa hand is another "protection symbol," and it comes from Islamic and also from Jewish tradition. In addition to dabbling with ecumenism with these symbols, professing Christians who wore these symbols would be showing faith in symbols to protect them instead of trusting in

God.
- **Organite pendants.** This is a clear resin poured mold, usually in a pyramid shape, that has copper shavings in it to supposedly protect people from electro-magnetic frequencies and "negative energy." Organite was invented by a lewd sex therapist and these items have no place in a Christian's life.
- **Celtic Knots, Spirals, and Vesica Piscis**: Often seen in New Age, Celtic, and Wiccan jewelry, Celtic knots and spirals symbolize eternity, interconnectedness, or even nature worship. While they can be connected to Irish traditions of marriage, these symbols can also be seen in pagan rituals or as representations of nature-based spirituality that doesn't acknowledge God as the Creator. For example, the Vesica Piscis symbol is vividly displayed at Glastonbury's Chalice Well, and is associated with the fish of Pisces. The Vesica Piscis symbol represents the union of opposites and the "divine feminine" which is integral to goddess worship.
- **Peace sign.** Some people believe that the peace symbol is an upside down broken cross, so it's therefore an anti-Christ symbol. Others argue that it's a representation of Peter being crucified upside down. Peace signs don't represent the true and lasting peace that only Jesus can give us. If a Christian's conscience isn't convicted by peace signs, then this could be a matter of Christian liberty. However, if other people notice you wearing a peace sign, you'll want to use it as an opportunity to share the Gospel so that the symbol doesn't cause them to stumble into believing in a works-based humanistic approach to peace.
- **Crystal points.** New agers and occultists believe that wearing or holding the point of a crystal will increase that person's psychic abilities.
- **Bohemian jewelry.** Bracelets or necklaces with charms that glorify mysticism or rebelliousness.

CHAPTER 5: NEW AGE JEWELRY TO REMOVE FROM YOUR HOME

- **Goddess and fertility pendants.** Instead of trusting God's will for childbearing, people will wear pendants of pagan female deities to try to conceive.
- **Astrological symbols or jewelry glorifying the moon or stars.** Since astrology is the condemned practice of divination and is serving God's creation (stars, moon, and planets) instead of the Creator, Christians should have nothing to do with astrology including jewelry with astrological symbols. And for those who try to justify astrology by claiming that the Magi were astrologers: it doesn't say that in the Bible. Jewelry that glorifies the moon or the stars is often associated with Wicca or witchcraft, which worships nature and believes in pantheism.
- **Co-Exist pendants.** The co-exist movement seems loving and kind on the surface, yet it's promoting the broad road instead of the narrow way. The truth is that these spiritual paths contradict each other, and they all contradict Christianity. Most importantly, Jesus proclaimed that He is the *only* way to God the Father (John 14:6).
- **Yoga and New Age meditation symbols on jewelry.** These include images of people meditating sitting in a lotus position similar to a Buddha; the Hindu elephant-headed deity Ganesha; the Ohm symbol; and the lotus flower. Yoga is not "just stretching" - it's an unredeemable Hindu worship practice including so-called "holy yoga." Non-yoga Pilates is a better choice for Christians. The symbols of meditation are also not Biblical, as the Bible defines meditation as reading the Bible and uttering it aloud. Eastern and new age meditation, in contrast, is all about focusing upon the self.
- **Crystal beaded stretchy bracelets:** Crystal beads can be beautiful, yet we Christians need to be aware of the loaded symbology in those stretchy elasticized bracelets made of round crystal beads. Notice that they're mostly sold at new age shops and health food stores.

New Age jewelry has a "bohemian" feel, because it appropriates from Eastern Indian Hindu culture. If you're going to wear a stretchy crystal bracelet, perhaps consider adding a pendant charm to it with a Bible verse engraved on it.

- **Malas:** Malas consist of 108 beads plus a larger "guru bead" and a tassle. The Hinduism practice is to count the mala beads while you're meditating. New Agers wear these malas as necklaces, as it gives an air and appearance of someone who's enlightened. Of course, the only true enlightenment is realizing that we're all sinners in need of Jesus Christ as our Lord and Savior.
- **The Yin and Yang:** This ancient Chinese symbol represents balance and duality between opposing forces, such as light and darkness. While it may seem innocent, it reflects the belief that good and evil are in harmony and balance—an idea that contradicts Scripture. 1 John 1:5 says: *"God is light, and in him is no darkness at all."* There is no "balance" between good and evil in God's kingdom because light drives out darkness. The new age falsely encourages people to "embrace your shadows" instead of repenting. Wearing the yin and yang symbol could subtly suggest that opposing forces can coexist in harmony, which isn't the biblical view.
- **Tibetan Buddhist necklaces.** My husband owned a few of these that we'd purchased in antique stores during our travels. The necklaces were brass or bronze and had coral or turquoise stones. They looked great with the bohemian and Eastern Indian outfits that he wore, but as soon as we were both saved in 2017, the necklaces went into the dumpster as they promoted Buddhism and not God.
- **Ceremonial jewelry.** In the Wiccan and goddess worship movement, women wear jewelry for ceremonies. Often there's an intersecting or triple moon symbol in the middle of this jewelry with crystals on either side. She may wear this jewelry as a

CHAPTER 5: NEW AGE JEWELRY TO REMOVE FROM YOUR HOME

headband with the symbol placed between her eyes. Other ceremonial jewelry includes large crystal rings and bracelets, and Renaissance-style belts.

- **Native American spirituality appropriation.** I don't understand why the new age isn't criticized more for its blatant appropriation, borrowing, and twisting of various worldwide cultures. For example, the new age takes symbols from Native American spirituality and appropriates them as jewelry. I would think that this trivializing of a cultural symbol would be offensive, and it's definitely spiritually dangerous to Christians. This includes dream catcher necklaces and earrings (please see Chapter 3 for more about dream catchers).
- **Kabbalah symbols.** This is another example of the new age superficially counterfeiting another culture, and turning its symbols into jewelry. The Kabbalah is unbiblical mysticism related to Judaism, yet it's not Jewish in the same way as the Rabbinical publications such as the Talmud. Kabbalstic symbols on jewelry include a "tree of life" that's only slightly related to the Bible's Tree of Life. The Kabbalah teaches about a sephiroth tree which is a path of spiritual growth governed by "archangels" who aren't in the Bible (except for Michael). Christians should avoid mysticism, and that includes the Kabbalah and its symbols.

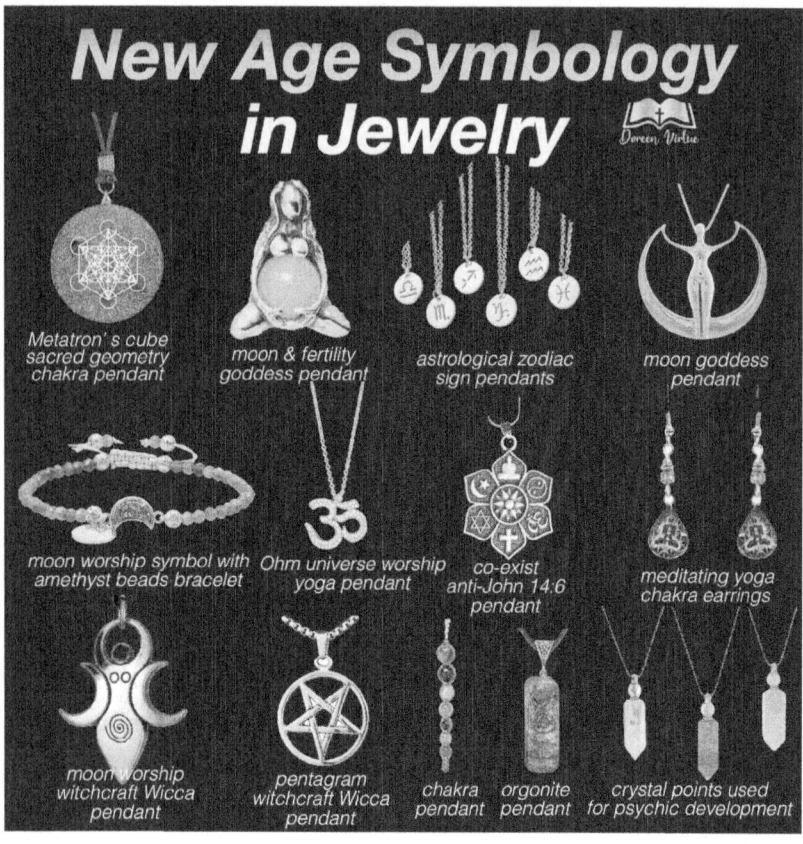

CHAPTER 5: NEW AGE JEWELRY TO REMOVE FROM YOUR HOME

"Christian" Jewelry That's Actually New Age

As Christians, we have liberty to wear jewelry that is either spiritually neutral or that glorifies God. For example, wearing a pendant with a Bible verse. Many Christians wear a cross pendant necklace or bracelet. I wear a small gold cross that my husband gave to me on the day that I was baptized. I find that it starts God-honoring conversations when people see me wearing the cross.

Some Christians are convicted to *not* wear a cross necklace. This is an example of following your conscience and the Holy Spirit's convictions.

However, if you do choose to wear a cross pendant, please make sure that it's actually a Christian cross which are usually plain with no decor on the cross. Please consult the chart below called "Not all crosses are Christian symbols" to see examples. You can research other examples online.

When I was raised in the Christian Science church, many people wore the "cross and crown" symbol of the religion. Then, when I was a new ager, I wore a cross from the Eastern Orthodox church because I liked the embellishments. I believed in the new age Jesus back then, which is the false Jesus. However, I didn't know that at the time, and I wore crosses to express my love for Jesus (particularly crosses made from crystals because I used crystals as new age idols back then).

Ironically, when my photo was shot for the cover of my new age heretical book, *The Lightworker's Way*, I wore a crystal cross pendant. Well, my former new age publisher was concerned about offending their audience, so they "air-brushed" or "photo-shopped" the cross out of my photo. Why I went along with that, I do not know.

Since I grew up in the 1970's, I'd always had a bohemian wardrobe style and that included Southwestern clothing. I had some Southwestern jackets with what I thought were Christian crosses on them. After being saved and while researching the symbols I had worn, I discovered that these were Native American "Spider Woman" goddess symbols and not Christian crosses. As much as I thought those jackets were beautiful artistry, I couldn't in good conscience promote goddess idolatry by wearing them - especially since I'd been tangled up in goddess worship before I was saved.

In the new age, I also wore pendants with images of Mother Mary because I was praying to her as if she was a goddess who could grant wishes. I also had pendants with images of elemental spirits such as mermaids and fairies. I disposed of those pendants as soon as I was saved by God in 2017. This is something for you to pray about for your

CHAPTER 5: NEW AGE JEWELRY TO REMOVE FROM YOUR HOME

own jewelry collection, as well.

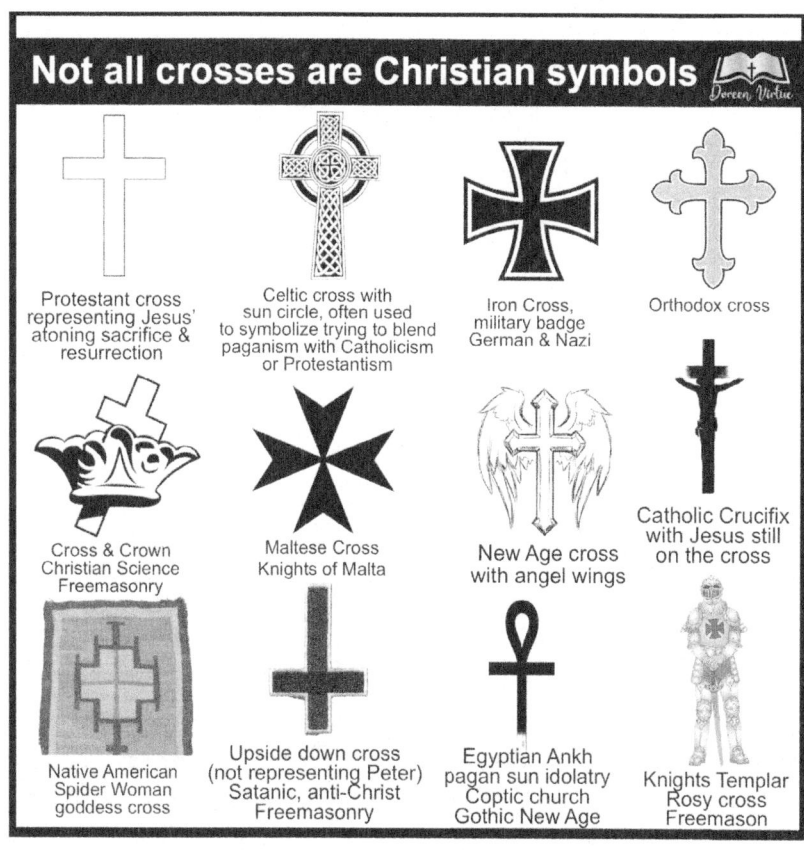

Some jewelry items may subtly communicate spiritual messages or ideas that contradict God's truth. For example, a cross pendant with angel wings is a new age symbol of idolatry and angel worship. So, please be prayerfully discerning.

Matthew 5:14-16 teaches us that we are the light of the world, and our lives should point others to Jesus. That means our jewelry shouldn't cause confusion or lead others into deception.

In addition, 1 Peter 3:3-4 says:

> "Your beauty should not come from outward adornment, such as elaborate hairstyles and the wearing of gold jewelry or fine clothes. Rather, it should be that of your inner self, the unfading beauty of a gentle and quiet spirit, which is of great worth in God's sight."

Our beauty is ultimately from the inside, and while wearing jewelry isn't wrong, we should make sure that it isn't pridefully drawing attention to ourselves or to things that could be spiritually harmful.

Romans 12:2 exhorts us:

> "Do not conform to the pattern of this world, but be transformed by the renewing of your mind."

If we wear jewelry with new age symbols, we might unintentionally be conforming to the world's trendy and dangerous spiritual mindset, which is not rooted in God's truth. Wearing symbols that represent things outside of God's kingdom can send the wrong message, both to ourselves and to others. We're called to live in a way that reflects the light of Christ, and that means avoiding anything that could cause us or others to stumble into spiritual confusion or deception.

In the room-by-room checklist, you may wonder why "kitchen" and "bathroom" are listed in the jewelry section. Well, some people have necklaces as wall hangings, and some people keep their jewelry boxes in their bathroom. The point is to prayerfully scour your home.

Checklist for Removing New Age Jewelry from Your Home

O n the next page, you'll see a checklist to use if you'd like, when walking through your home to find and remove new age jewelry. Be sure to check your garage, closets, drawers, attic, basement, suitcases, purses, coat pockets, and even outdoor spaces.

REMOVING NEW AGE FROM YOUR HOME

KITCHEN
-
-
-
-
-
-
-

LIVING ROOM
-
-
-
-
-
-

HALLWAY / ENTRY
-
-
-
-
-
-
-

BEDROOM
-
-
-
-
-

OTHER
-
-
-
-
-
-
-

BATHROOM
-
-
-
-
-
-

Chapter 6: New Age Clothing to Remove from Your Home

Similar to the new age jewelry that we discussed in Chapter 5, so should our clothing either be neutral or glorifying to God - and definitely not glorifying darkness.

In this chapter, we'll address clothing with New Age or occultic symbols. Just like jewelry or artwork, the clothes we wear can carry messages and have spiritual significance and could influence people who see them.

As Christians, we're called to be mindful of what we wear, not only because it represents us to the world, but also because other people could be influenced by what they see us wearing. Most students of the Bible know that God exhorts us to dress modestly. Yet, God's condemnation of paganism, divination, and idolatry also applies to our clothing choices.

We're going to discuss how to identify clothing with New Age and occultic symbols, and why it's important to remove these items from your wardrobe. We'll also describe clothing that may be used in Wiccan or witchcraft ceremonies, and address the topic of cosplay, Halloween, and Renaissance costumes.

The Bible says that everything we do should glorify God. Glorifying God is our purpose. Wearing clothing with occultic or New Age symbols, even unintentionally, doesn't glorify God.

I once spoke with a young man who was wearing a sweatshirt that had a large image of the tarot "death" card on it. This man said that he had no idea of the symbolic meaning of the card, and that he'd just bought it because he thought it looked cool. When I shared the Gospel with him and cautioned him about the danger particularly of the "death" tarot card, he was visibly shaken. I've asked people, and now I ask you please, to pray for God to open his eyes and save him.

As Christians, we want to avoid t-shirts or hoodies with new age slogans like:

- "Manifest your dreams"
- "Cosmic vibes only"
- "The universe has your back"
- "Namaste all day"
- "Energy flows where attention goes"
- "Awaken your spirit"

These phrases may seem positive or harmless, yet they reflect New Age teachings that elevate the universe or self above God. Wearing them is a silent endorsement and promotion of these beliefs.

The point is that a lot of people wear new age clothing, without realizing its significance. New age clothing is trendy and popular, and regular stores like Target and Walmart sell apparel with new age symbols - even for children.

New age symbols aren't neutral, as they come from pagan systems of belief that contradict God's truth. Here are some of the common symbols linked to New Age, occultic, or pagan practices that are often printed on tshirts and sweatshirt hoodies:

CHAPTER 6: NEW AGE CLOTHING TO REMOVE FROM YOUR HOME

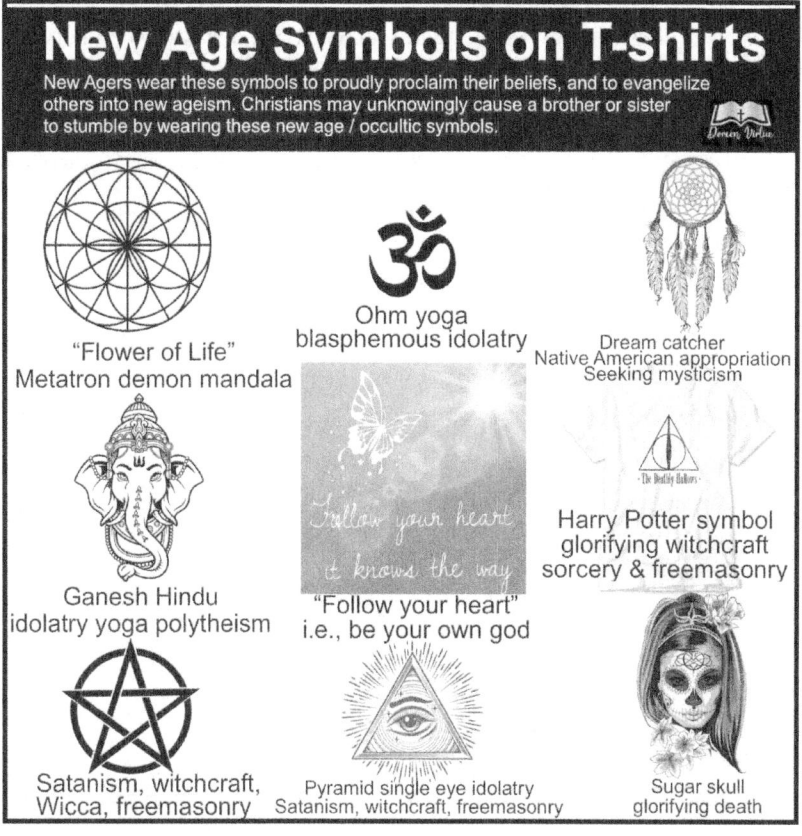

- **The Pentagram**: As mentioned earlier, the pentagram is a five-pointed star associated with witchcraft, Satanism, and occultic rituals. This symbol also appears on some "death metal" or heavy metal band shirts. While some people might wear it as a fashion statement, the symbol has a spiritual meaning, particularly within the Wiccan and satanic communities. Even when I was in the new age, I was repulsed by pentagrams and I stayed away from them. Pentagrams should *not* be worn by Christians.
- **Witchcraft and Satanic symbols**. Have you noticed how many people walk around these days with blatantly satanic symbols on

their shirts? I pray for them and look for opportunities to share the Gospel. Often, these are people who felt rejected by the local church and they're acting out their hurt feelings by rejecting the Gospel through anti-Christ beliefs. Please pray for them. As Christians, we wouldn't purposely wear any symbols of witchcraft or satanism. These symbols include an upside down cross; Triple moons with the new moon, crescent moon, and full moon; hexagram "seal of Solomon" (it's not representative of the Biblical accounts of King Solomon - it's a legend about how a ring with this symbol allowed Solomon to control the demons); Ouroboros image of a serpent or dragon eating its own tail; a horned deity; two crescent shapes representing horns; Triquetra which is three interlaced arcs or loops; Sigils which are abstract symbols that represent magical intentions. Usually these symbols are in red on black clothing.

- **Reiki symbols**. The new age "energy healing" system utilizes hand-drawn symbols that were part of a vision that Reiki's spiritualist Buddhist originator Mikao Usui had. To become a "Reiki master," you need to become "vibrationally attuned" to these symbols. Christians should have nothing to do with the strange fire of Reiki and similar energy healing systems.
- **The Ankh**: This ancient Egyptian symbol, which looks like a cross with a loop at the top, represents eternal life in Egyptian spirituality. It's sometimes seen on t-shirts and accessories in modern fashion, especially in New Age circles. While it may seem like a simple design, the ankh has spiritual ties to ancient Egyptian beliefs and is used in paganism and occult practices to symbolize life and death cycles outside of God's divine plan.
- **The Eye of Horus**: This symbol, often depicted as an eye inside a triangle, is associated with protection and spiritual enlightenment in Egyptian mysticism and is commonly used in occult circles. This symbol is linked to the worship of Horus, an Egyptian god. Wearing

CHAPTER 6: NEW AGE CLOTHING TO REMOVE FROM YOUR HOME

this symbol, whether consciously or not, may invite the spiritual influence tied to this belief system. One-eyed symbols like the Eye of Horus are connected to Freemasonry and satanic symbolism. It represents a belief in unseen spiritual forces and the search for hidden knowledge, which was the devil's promise to Eve that led her and Adam to sin in the Garden.

- **"Sacred Geometry" also known as Metatron's Cube, Mandala, Chakra, or Flower of Life.** In the new age, there's a belief that God's symmetry in creation is a key to mystical knowledge. This is symbolized as a circle containing geometric shapes. Sometimes, it's credited to an "archangel" who's in the Kabbalah and not in the Bible named Metatron. I used to believe in him, but I now believe that it's another example of a demon masquerading as an angel in order to deceive people. Geometric shapes don't enlighten us - God's Word is our source of wisdom.
- **Skulls and Tattoo Art.** As Christians, we are to glorify God. Skull images or gory images glorify death and darkness. The edgy Gothic style of most tattoo art also glorifies a gloomy, angry, and dark approach to life, instead of embracing the Fruit of the Spirit such as peace and joy. This may be a matter of Christian liberty, yet it's something to be prayed about because these symbols could also cause others to stumble.
- **Images of Drugs or Alcohol.** While Christians can drink alcohol in moderation, drunkenness or being stoned are sins because the Bible tells us to be sober-minded and alert to the devil's schemes. So, we wouldn't want to promote over-indulgance by wearing images that promote drugs or alcohol.
- **Foul Language or Immorality.** In the secular world, people curse and display loose morals. Yet we Christians are held to a sanctified "set apart" standard through the warnings in God's Word. We're exhorted not to cuss and to live a life of integrity and monogamy.

So, we wouldn't want to glorify worldly ways with such images on our t-shirts.
- **Second or Third Commandment Violations, or Disrespect to God's Word.** A Christian wouldn't want to wear a t-shirt that uses the Lord's name in vain - including the popular OMG phrase, or that portrays a disrespectful image of Jesus or any Bible story.
- **Images of Sorcerers or Witches.** If it glorifies sorcery or witchcraft, it has to go. This includes t-shirts or hoodies with images of Harry Potter or Harry Potter characters, sorcerers from Lord of the Rings, witches from Wicked, and so forth. We only glorify God, and not what God condemns - even if those characters seem "lovable."
- **Death Metal Band Merch.** Do the lyrics from the death metal band glorify God? If not, why would we want to promote them by wearing their shirts, if their lyrics glorify darkness?
- **The Yin and Yang**: This symbol represents the belief in balancing opposing forces in the universe. This symbol was highly popular in the 1970's. Today, the belief is more apt to be expressed as, "Embrace your shadow side" as it reflects the Eastern mystical belief in balance between good and evil, which is a contradiction to the truth in 1 John 1:5 that "God is light; in Him, there is no darkness at all." So, wearing this symbol could inadvertently support the Eastern and new age idea of relativism, where evil and good are equal, necessary and defined by subjective opinions - which directly opposes the Gospel truth that Jesus died to save us from the punishment for our sins.
- **Symbols of Nature Worship**: God made nature, yet new agers worship God's creation instead of the Creator. Items of clothing featuring trees, moons, sun symbols, a Green Man image, or mystical power animals - especially when combined with new age symbols - can be tied to this belief system. The symbolism may

CHAPTER 6: NEW AGE CLOTHING TO REMOVE FROM YOUR HOME

also borrow from Native American beliefs in "power animals" and feature wolves, eagles, or jaguars combined with mystical images. Nature worship tries to elevate the created world above the Creator, which is contrary to the biblical call to worship God alone. This is related to the unbiblical belief in pantheism, which is believing that God is within the trees, rocks, and so forth. God is the creator of nature, yet the Bible clearly says that He's separate from His creation. Wearing nature worship symbols can communicate a subtle connection to beliefs that treat nature as sacred, rather than acknowledging God as the Creator of all.

Yoga Clothing

I did daily yoga for over 20 years before I was saved, and so I speak from experience and research here: Yoga poses (*asanas* in Sanskrit) are a Hindu pagan worship practice, in which you twist your body into a graven image of one of the 330 million pagan deities in Hinduism. The ancient Hindu books all explain this, and Hindus can't understand why Christians would ever choose to do yoga. It's not "just stretching" - it's an unredeemable pagan worship practice.

Stretching is very important, and so now as a Christian I do non-yoga Pilates using a Pilates reformer that I've owned for many years. You can purchase an inexpensive used Pilates reformer for yourself.

I have videos on the topic of why Christians shouldn't do yoga on my YouTube.com/@Doreen_Virtue channel and also wrote about why yoga isn't redeemable (even so-called "holy yoga") in my book, *How to Avoid New Age & New Thought Deception*.

There's another issue with yoga, and that's modesty. I spent two decades inside of yoga studios and most yoga clothing isn't modest. There's skin-tight yoga pants and cropped yoga tops. In some classes, such as "hot yoga" it's common for women and men to wear extremely small shorts called "bootie shorts."

I know that yoga pants are comfortable, yet we need to practice modesty as Christian women. If we wear leggings, our bottoms need to be covered by a long top. We don't want to cause a brother to stumble into lust by provocatively showing our body in tight clothing.

> "But I say to you that everyone who looks at a woman with lustful intent has already committed adultery with her in his heart." Matthew 5:28
>
> "Likewise also that women should adorn themselves in respectable apparel, with modesty and self-control" 1 Timothy 2:9

Most yoga clothing are decorated with symbols from Hinduism, the occult, or new ageism. Some common yoga symbols include:

- An elephant to represent the pagan deity Ganesha
- A lotus flower to represent an open heart chakra energy center
- Chakras or mandala geometric circles which are tied to the Hindu belief that we're controlled by energy centers
- Hindu Sanskrit words such as "Namaste" (which is translated into a blasphemous message)
- The Hindu Sanskrit symbol for Om or Ahm which is believed to represent universal energy (instead of putting our belief and faith in God)
- A silhouetted figure of a person meditating in a lotus position (this is not like Biblical meditation)
- Images of Hindu or Buddhist goddesses
- A Hamsa hand from Islamic culture which is supposed to ward off evil (instead of turning to God for protection)
- Tree of Life from the Jewish mystic Kabbalah (not the Tree of Life from the Bible)
- Yin-Yang symbol representing balance of dark and light (when the

Bible tells us that light overcomes darkness)

I threw these items of clothing away after I was saved, along with my yoga mats because they also had pagan symbols on them.

Clothing Used in Wiccan, Goddess Worship, and Witchcraft Ceremonies

In addition to symbols, Christians should avoid clothing associated with witchcraft or Wiccan ceremonies. Some items are directly used in rituals or are identified with witchcraft culture, and wearing these could inadvertently promote occult practices.

- **Black Cloaks and Robes**: Wicca and various witchcraft traditions often include black cloaks, robes, or hoods as part of their ceremonial dress. These items represent mystery, protection, and the spiritual world. Remember that the devil tries to lure people to follow him, by promising access to secrets and hidden knowledge. Yet, the devil is the father of lies who can't impart any truth or wisdom.
- **Goddess Gowns.** These floor-length gowns were a staple of my wardrobe when I was giving new age workshops. Usually, they were made of purple stretch velvet with a Gothic or Renaissance style. They were immodest because they were usually form-fitting with plunging necklines. They had trumpet, flare, or bell sleeves, with the fabric around the wrists open larger than the upper sleeves. In ceremonial rituals, the trumpet sleeves are supposed to conduct "energy." These gowns are a way to imitate and glorify goddesses and the so-called "divine feminine energy," instead of glorifying God our Creator. I was frequently in Glastonbury, England which is a witchcraft capital and home to a goddess temple which I

frequented, and nearly every woman there wore these velvet gowns.
- **Altar Clothes**: Some clothing items are part of Wiccan or witchcraft altar rituals, such as aprons, shawls, or ceremonial robes. These items are also part of the theatrics of rituals as they attempt to invoke spirits (demons) and cast spells.
- **Elements of Witchcraft Symbols on Clothing**: Wiccan and witchcraft practitioners often wear clothing with symbols like the triple moon, which represents the goddess and the cycle of the moon. The pentacle (as discussed earlier), a circle with a five-pointed star, is another common symbol found on Wiccan attire. If these symbols appear on shirts, dresses, or other garments, they should be discarded, as they glorify witchcraft.

The main reason to remove clothing with occultic or New Age symbols is because we're set apart for God's purposes. 2 Corinthians 6:14 says:

> *"Do not be yoked together with unbelievers. For what do righteousness and wickedness have in common? Or what fellowship can light have with darkness?"*

We're also called to live in a way that glorifies God and reflects His holiness. Romans 12:1 tells us to offer our bodies as "a living sacrifice, holy and pleasing to God." This includes how we present ourselves in the world. By wearing clothing that represents occultic beliefs, we promote darkness instead of the true saving Gospel of Jesus Christ.

Cosplay, Renaissance, and Halloween Costumes

Before we were saved, my husband and I were actively involved with wearing Cosplay costumes to ComicCon Expos, Medieval costumes at Renaissance Fairs (RenFaires), and Halloween costumes based upon

CHAPTER 6: NEW AGE CLOTHING TO REMOVE FROM YOUR HOME

movie characters like superheroes.

When we were saved in 2017, my husband threw away the costumes even though they were expensive and some might say that they were harmless. This is an example of Christian liberty yielding to the Holy Spirit's convictions which may look different for each person.

Let's consider various types of costumes, and some principles to weigh your decision about whether or not to wear or keep them:

Renaissance & Medieval Costumes

RenFaires can feel like you're stepping back in time through the decor, costumes, and role playing. Participants usually wear historically inspired costumes, engage in role-playing as if they were in the middle ages, and partake in themed entertainment. There are also clubs for live-action role playing (LARP) and recreating the culture of the Middle Ages such as the Society for Creative Anachronism (SCA).

Cosplay usually involves attending a ComicCon Expo while dressed as a fictional character, such as super heroes and heroines, or characters from comic books, anime, video games, or movies. This usually involves elaborate and expensive costumes, makeup, wigs, and even adopting character mannerisms.

RenFaires and Cosplay can be a fun form of creative expression, social interaction, and developing an appreciation of art and history. Yet, I also remember RenFaire attendees chugging pints of beer and groping at scantily clad women. The heart of biblical modesty is humility, self-control, and a focus on godliness rather than outward appearance that draws lewd attention or promotes pride.

Most RenFaires have fortune-tellers in booths, which promotes the condemned practice of divination. They often have booths selling witchcraft tools and items which glorify paganism. We'd always leave the RenFaires before the sun went down, to avoid the loud, lewd, and often dangerous drunkenness of some of the attendees that's especially prevalent at night.

Role-playing in itself isn't inherently evil. However, Christians should have nothing to do with cosplay that involves:

- Characters associated with witchcraft, occultism, or dark spiritual forces,
- Environments or events promoting occult rituals or demonic themes,
- Personal involvement in practices contrary to God's Word

We haven't attended a ComicCon Expo or RenFaire since we left the new age for Christ. These activities don't attract us anymore. We believe there's Christian liberty in whether or not someone attends these functions or dresses in these costumes. And there are definitely opportunities to share the Gospel at these events!

As always, the questions about whether these costumes or activities are appropriate for Christians include:

- Do these activities and the costumes glorify God?
- Is the RenFaire or ComicCon an appropriate atmosphere for a Christian?
- Are the costumes modest, or do they promote lust or other sins?
- Have I allowed the characters that I'm role-playing or the costumes to become idols to me?
- What's the nature of the character or theme I'm portraying?
- Does this character glorify God or promote a worldview opposed to biblical truth?
- Am I wearing this costume to glorify God, or to attract worldly attention to myself?
- Do the costumes or activities glorify sorcery, witchcraft, divination, or idolatry?

CHAPTER 6: NEW AGE CLOTHING TO REMOVE FROM YOUR HOME

These costumes can also be expensive and time-consuming to research, create, make or purchase. I remember spending hours researching how my cosplay "character" looked so that I could mimic the details. Then, I spent time and money resourcing the elements of the costume, or purchasing a ready-made costume. So, this is another question for Christians to consider:

- Is this a good use of the financial and time provision with which God has blessed us?

The bottom-line is to pray for God's wisdom and then to obey the Holy Spirit's convictions if He guides you to throw away your costumes and/or to stop participating in cosplay. Prayerful discernment and wise counsel from mature Christians can help us determine if specific cosplay or costumes might expose her to harmful spiritual influences.

Ultimately, Christians are called to glorify God in everything they do:

> "So, whether you eat or drink, or whatever you do, do all to the glory of God." 1 Corinthians 10:31

Halloween Costumes

Costumes that glorify death, gore, witchcraft, sorcery or other forms of sin or darkness don't belong in a Christian's home. Most Christians agree that Halloween is a celebration of paganism, so they choose alternatives such as celebrating the anniversary of Martin Luther's reformation post on October 31, 1517. Or, they hold "harvest festivals" at their church. Halloween is also a ripe occasion to distribute Gospel tracts and pray for the lost.

It would be questionable for a Christian to keep any costume that promotes something that the Bible condemns. Halloween costumes, decorations, and props to avoid would include anything that glorifies darkness, the occult, the devil, or death such as:

- Witch costumes including witch hats
- Satanic and devil themed costumes or accessories
- Witch cauldrons
- Ghouls, ghosts, demons, or goblins
- Divination decorations such as a Ouija board, tarot cards, or crystal ball decor
- Violent or gory costumes or decorations
- Fortune-teller costumes or decorations
- Sorcery costumes, including Harry Potter themes
- Costumes that mock Christianity
- Immodest provocative costumes that promote lust
- Costumes of ungodly immoral characters

If you have any of these items in your home, it's advisable to throw them away or burn them. You wouldn't sell or donate these items, because you don't want them to cause someone else to stumble into glorifying darkness.

What About Bohemian Clothing?

Before I was saved, most of my clothing was either Renaissance, Gothic, or Bohemian themed. The term "Bohemian" refers to its association with free-spirited nomadic artists, writers, and musicians who wore second-hand and unconventional clothing because they rejected social norms and were counter-cultural. Sometimes this style is shorted to "boho" and it continues to evoke a sense of fierce independence and rebelliousness. It's also associated with a new age worldview.

CHAPTER 6: NEW AGE CLOTHING TO REMOVE FROM YOUR HOME

I grew up in the 1960's and 1970's when the Beatles had ushered in Eastern Indian influences. At first, it was the "flower child" era of Haight-Ashbury in 1967 and then it segued into the "hippie era" of Woodstock in 1969. It seemed like everyone wore block print clothing from India in the late 1960's and into the 1970's! They were a status symbol in that era.

Bohemian clothing also included tie-dye shirts and dresses, flower-power images, headbands, and cottage core Gunne Sax dresses. Bohemian clothing is often a symbol of rejecting societal norms and embracing a spirituality that's detached from God. Many in the hippie movement were influenced by beliefs like pantheism (the belief that God is in everything), occult practices, and the exploration of drugs as a spiritual experience. These beliefs conflict with the biblical worldview, which teaches that God is separate from His creation and that true peace comes through faith in Christ alone (John 14:27).

Bohemian clothing is associated with drug abuse, New Age, promiscuity, rebelliousness, and occultic influences. There's a free-spirited "hippie" sense to these styles. Those who wore Bohemian styles in the 60's and 70's lived however they wanted to, without a moral compass. Living in communes, attending orgies, being stoned on drugs all day, listening to rock music, and quitting college were the "values" that hippies embraced.

Bohemian clothing can be symbolic of rejecting conservative values and embracing a do-it-yourself spiritual path. Many in the 1970's hippie movement were influenced by beliefs like Eastern Indian gurus and Hinduism, pantheism (the belief that God is in everything), taking LSD and believing their "acid trip" gave them profound revelations, occult practices, and the exploration of drugs as a spiritual experience. These beliefs conflict with the biblical worldview, which teaches that God is separate from His creation and that true peace comes through faith in Christ alone (John 14:27).

In addition to growing up in the hippie era, my fashion tastes were influenced by the Bohemian wardrobe of singer Stevie Nicks. I first saw Stevie in concert in the 1970's when she was with Fleetwood Mac, and I was mesmerized by her flowing diaphanous gowns and fringed scarves. Stevie glorifies witchcraft, goddess worship, feminism, and abortion with her songs and interviews, though, so I wouldn't want to emulate her in any way these days. Instead, I pray for her.

Additionally, tie-dye fashion is sometimes linked to ideas of Reiki healing, chakra alignment, goddess worship, and other spiritual deception - concepts that are far removed from the truths of the Bible. When I was a new ager, I bought some of my Bohemian and tie-die clothing from independent sellers on Etsy. Many of them were openly involved with new age and occultic practices. They even hand-stamped symbols on the dresses that they made for me, such as gold metallic chakra mandalas. I thought they were cool at the time, but they went into the dumpster after I was saved.

When we were first saved, my husband and I wore this type of clothing to church because that's all we owned. Yet, we noticed that we alone wore loud colorful prints to church. Most others in the congregation wore subdued prints and conservative styles. To their credit, there wasn't any partiality at our church, even though we stood out with our hippie clothing styles and my husband's longish hair. We soon stopped wanting to wear our Bohemian styles. My husband cut his hair and we dressed more conservatively.

There's some Christian liberty in this area. I still think that some bohemian clothing is cute as long as it's modest. Yet, we don't want to cause anyone to stumble by wearing clothing that has occultic symbols or that could convey "follow your heart" instead of obedience to God. So, this would be a matter between your conscience and the Holy Spirit's leading.

CHAPTER 6: NEW AGE CLOTHING TO REMOVE FROM YOUR HOME

Removing New Age and Occultic Clothing

Here are some practical steps to take in removing new age and occultic influences from your wardrobe:

- Pray for God's wisdom and leading as you examine your clothing. Using the Holy Spirit's guidance and convictions and the information in this chapter, separate any clothing that needs to go. Put that clothing into large trash bags.
- Repent for your previous clothing choices.
- Remove the new age and occultic clothing from your home (which includes your garage). Either toss it in the trash or burn it. Please don't donate or sell the clothing, as we don't want to pass along these influences.
- Pray for God's discernment, wisdom, and leading in your future clothing purchases. Pray that your clothing is God-honoring and reflects your identity in Christ. Perhaps you may want to acquire and wear t-shirts printed with your favorite Bible verses. These are wonderful ways to open a conversation so that you can share the Gospel.
- Christian-themed clothing and jewelry can be a blessing when they point clearly to the gospel and biblical truth. But avoid: Designs that mix Bible verses with New Age imagery; Bible verses taken out-of-context to imply that God is a wish-granter; Crosses that are heavily stylized or combined with other spiritual symbols; Items that promote a "feel-good" Christianity without repentance or faith.

Always ask: *Does this glorify God and align with Scripture?*

The clothes we wear are more than a fashion choice - they're an expression of what we believe. Choosing to remove occult or New

Age symbols from your wardrobe is a bold act of submission to God's authority. It's not about legalism but about loving God with your whole mind, heart, and body.

In Chapter 7, we'll clear out any books or other printed materials that are new age or which promote false teachings.

Checklist for Removing New Age Clothing from Your Home

Here's a checklist to use, if you'd like, when walking through your home to find and remove new age clothing. Be sure to check your garage, closets, drawers, suitcases, attic, basement, and even outdoor spaces.

REMOVING NEW AGE FROM YOUR HOME

KITCHEN	LIVING ROOM
☐	☐
☐	☐
☐	☐
☐	☐
☐	☐
☐	☐
☐	☐

HALLWAY / ENTRY	BEDROOM
☐	☐
☐	☐
☐	☐
☐	☐
☐	☐
☐	☐
☐	☐

OTHER	BATHROOM
☐	☐
☐	☐
☐	☐
☐	☐
☐	☐
☐	☐
☐	☐

Chapter 7: New Age and False Gospel Books to Remove from Your Home

New age, new thought, and occult books and magazines promise to reveal secret hidden wisdom in their pages. This promise of secret wisdom is the same lure that the serpent used to hook Eve in the Garden. New Thought (positive thinking to get what you want) and New age/occultic beliefs (conjuring, "manifesting," divination, or spirit communication with tools or rituals) are often woven into books about health; grief recovery; cook books; managing finances; relationships; and self-help topics.

New age, new thought, and the occult are all do-it-yourself systems. They teach people to use their own power and strength to make things happen, instead of turning to God and trusting His will and His timing. So, the books that we're purging from your home are all do-it-yourself spirituality.

As Christians we want to make sure that we don't have any new age, new thought or occultic books in our homes. If something happened to you, would your family members find and be influenced by these books? Would they mistakenly think that you believed what was in these books? You don't want to leave a legacy of spiritual deception.

So, let's do a deep dive into the books which you have, in order to clear them out of your home. Here are some examples of book topics and genres which don't belong in a Christian home. You'll find additional details in the other chapters in this book about why these topics contradict the Bible and don't belong in Christian homes.

This list is not exhaustive, as there are many topics which contradict the Bible, and the devil invents new forms of deception all the time. So, this list is a good jumping off place to begin in cleaning deception out of your home:

Alchemy / Spiritual Alchemy - Although it was originally tied to medieval chemistry, alchemy is now an occultic tool for manifesting abundance. It promotes a mystical path to enlightenment and materialism that contradicts Scripture.

Aliens / UFOs / E.T.s - Obsession with extraterrestrial beings can distract from biblical truths and lead to speculative theology. ET's are demons and their crafts are demonic deceptions that are either made by humans or by demons.

Astrology / Horoscopes - Astrology attributes guidance and personal destiny to the stars and the planets, rather than to God's sovereign will. It promotes a worldview that contradicts biblical teachings about God's control over creation and the future. And no, the Magi weren't astrologers.

Astral Projection / Out-of-Body Experiences - Attempting to separate the soul from the body for spiritual experiences is not only unbiblical but can also be spiritually dangerous.

Automatic Writing / Spirit Writing - This practice involves going into a trance and surrendering one's mind or hand to external forces to receive messages. It's dangerous because it bypasses rational thought and spiritual discernment, making it an open door to demonic influence.

CHAPTER 7: NEW AGE AND FALSE GOSPEL BOOKS TO REMOVE FROM...

The Bible tells us to be alert and sober-minded because the devil seeks inattentive people to devour.

Chakra Balancing / Chakra Clearing - These practices are Hindu and based in clairvoyance and a belief that internal "energy wheels" determine our health and destiny, instead of acknowledging our sovereign God.

Channeled Books - Channeled books claim to contain secret hidden wisdom from spirits, which contradict the authority of Scripture. The reality is that these books have agendas to point people away from Jesus and Bible study. And no, the Bible isn't a "channeled book" - it is the God-breathed all-sufficient and inerrant Word of God.

Contemplative Practices / Lectio Divina / Centering Prayer / Breathwork - Though often framed as Christian, these practices can open the door to mystical experiences rooted in non-biblical meditation methods. They emphasize emptying the mind and going into trances, rather than filling it with God's Word. They also encourage trying to receive "messages" while in the trance, which is spiritually dangerous.

Crystals for idolatry, healing therapy, divination, psychic development - Using crystals for healing or spiritual power places trust in created objects rather than in the Creator. This can become a form of idolatry or occult practice, both of which Scripture warns against. Crystals are fine if they're only appreciated as beautiful creations from God, and not used in idolatrous or divination ways.

Curses / Generational Curses Teaching - While the Bible describes that the consequences of sin affect generations, modern generational curse teachings can promote fear and legalism. They distort Scripture and promote unbiblical "deliverance ministries" or self-deliverance by overemphasizing "Jesus gave us authority" out-of-context. Most human problems come from unrepentant sin, the consequences of prior sin, or God allowing us to suffer so that we'll grow closer to Him. We need to repent and take responsibility rather than blaming our problems on "generational curses."

Divination Instructions - Divination using cards, pendulums, and other new age tools to try to peak into the future promise that they'll give people hidden knowledge through supernatural means other than God, which directly violates Deuteronomy 18:10–12. Divination is a lack of trust in God's will, timing, and provision.

Dream Interpreting - While dreams appear in Scripture, modern dream interpretation practices are often rooted in New Age or occult methods. These interpretations are inconsistent and speculative, often replacing Scripture with human reasoning, wishful thinking, or even demonic deception.

Elemental Spirits / Fairies / Unicorns / Mermaids - Fascination with mythical beings can lead to an unhealthy obsession with fantasy, spiritual beings, and trances that do not glorify God. Some traditions link these creatures to occult or pagan systems. Demons can masquerade as elemental spirits, so caution is needed.

Enneagram - Though popular in some Christian circles, the Enneagram has occultic and mystical origins and is based on esoteric teachings and automatic writing, not psychology or Scripture. It can become a prideful identity source that competes with and contradicts biblical truth. Our identity is in Christ, not in an Enneagram number.

CHAPTER 7: NEW AGE AND FALSE GOSPEL BOOKS TO REMOVE FROM...

Energy Healing / Reiki / Pranic Healing / Hands of Light - These practices involve channeling unseen energy forces, which is spiritually dangerous. They bypass prayer and biblical healing, promoting trust in mystical powers rather than in God. These methods may sometimes seem to work, yet they lead people further into new age deception.

Feng Shui - Feng Shui is based on Taoist beliefs and attempts to control one's environment through spiritual energy flow by rearranging furniture and adding items such as mirrors and crystals. It places faith in forces outside God's sovereignty and contradicts biblical stewardship and trust.

Goddess Worship / Divine Feminine Spirituality / Feminine Empowerment - These ideologies often reject the biblical view of God and human identity, promoting self-exaltation that women are superior to men. This is often a rejection of Christianity because it is patriarchal. The worship of deities violates the First Commandment and is also spiritually dangerous.

Health or Cook Books that Incorporate New Age Beliefs - Books that promise supernatural healing, secret wisdom, or New Age healing methods combined with a focus upon health or food. This is often couched as a hidden "truth" instead of pointing to Jesus, Who is the Truth.

Kundalini Awakening - This Eastern practice seeks to awaken a serpent-like energy at the base of the spine, which is rooted in Hinduism. It is incompatible with the indwelling of the Holy Spirit and is spiritually dangerous because it opens participants to demonic influence.

Law of Attraction / Manifesting / Name-it-and-Claim-it / Decree

& Declare / The Secret / Prosperity Gospel - These teachings emphasize self-will and human words over God's will and Word. It's a do-it-yourself approach to acquiring, instead of trusting God's provision and sufficiency. They present a distorted view of faith, often blending prosperity theology with New Age principles. Some of these books suggest that people command God to give them things by "decreeing and declaring." Even worse, some of the authors say that if you send them money that God will bless you with wealth. This is conjuring, which is the condemned practice of sorcery.

Lucid Dreaming - Seeking to control dreams for spiritual experiences can cross into occult or mystical territory. It can encourage reliance on altered states rather than upon God's Word and prayer.

Mandala Coloring Books - Mandalas originate from the Hindu belief in chakra energy wheels, and are often used in meditation to reach altered states of consciousness. Engaging with them for spiritual purposes can lead to trances which dangerously opens people up to deception and an increased appetite for more New Age teachings.

Meditation Instructions - Eastern or New Age - Eastern and New Age meditation seeks to empty the mind and connect with an impersonal force, which contrasts with biblical meditation that fills the mind with God's Word. This practice can lead to spiritual vulnerability and confusion. 'Mindfulness' is the unbiblical practice of noticing your thoughts without judgment, while the Bible teaches to take every thought captive and Jesus explained that sinful thoughts are equivalent to sinful actions.

Near-Death Experiences - Near-death accounts often contradict the Bible's clear teaching on death, judgment, and the afterlife, and promote universalism. These stories of heaven also contradict each other. Trust should rest in God's Word, not in subjective and often contradictory personal experiences.

Numerology / Angel Numbers / Birth Numbers / Bible Numbers - These New Age systems assign mystical meanings to numbers. It's a form of the condemned and dangerous practice of divination that competes with trusting in God's sovereignty. Beware also of authors who claim to have "cracked the code" on repeating numbers or Hebrew letters in the Bible. The Bible never gives the meaning for repeating numbers, so this is extra-biblical speculation. Also, the Bible's chapter and verse numbers were added in the 1500's and are not divinely inspired.

Occultic Books / Ancient Egyptian Spirituality / Hermeticism / Grimoires - These texts promote beliefs and practices contrary to Christianity, often glorifying gods and rituals condemned in Scripture. Engaging with such materials can lead to further spiritual deception.

Paganism - Paganism worships nature as pantheists (believing that God and the universe are identical) and also worships multiple deities instead of the one true God revealed in Scripture. The *belief* in multiple dieties is called *henotheism*, and the *worship* of multiple deities is called *polytheism*. This includes the new age belief in "ascended masters" or "the great white brotherhood." These practices are condemned in the Bible, are spiritually dangerous, and are incompatible with Christian monotheism.

Past-Life Regression / Reincarnation - These teachings deny the biblical truth that "it is appointed unto man once to die, and then the judgment" Hebrews 9:27. They promote a Hindu cyclical view of life rather than eternal destiny through Christ. If we could reincarnate instead of repent, why did Jesus have to die on the cross for our sins?

Prosperity Gospel / Name It and Claim It - A "Christianized" version of the new age Law of Attraction, in which it's falsely taught that God will open a storehouse of riches if we tithe enough or decree and declare in the right way. Television pastors are usually the authors of these blasphemous books which portray God as a genie instead of as our Creator that we must fear and worship.

Psychic Development Instructions - Developing psychic abilities is forbidden in Scripture, as it involves contacting spirits or gaining hidden knowledge through unbiblical means. This practice is spiritually dangerous and misleading.

Sacred Geometry - This New Age concept treats certain shapes as holding divine power or spiritual significance. It reflects a mystical worldview that attributes spiritual power to creation instead of the Creator.

Sacred Texts of Other Religions Used Devotionally - Using texts like the Bhagavad Gita, the Quran, or Buddhist Sutras for spiritual growth undermines the sufficiency of Scripture. Christians are called to be discerning and not mix truth with error. Beware of the fallacy of believing that ancient teachings must be true, because the age of a teaching isn't a measure of its accuracy - the Bible is the measure.

Shamanism / Spirit Animals / Power Animals / Plant Spirit Medicine - These practices are rooted in animism and spiritism, which involve invoking spiritual entities other than God. They're incompatible with biblical Christianity and considered forms of idolatry or

CHAPTER 7: NEW AGE AND FALSE GOSPEL BOOKS TO REMOVE FROM...

occultism.

Sound Baths / Frequency Healing / Binaural Beats / Crystal Bowls Instruction Books - These practices claim to heal or align the body and spirit through sound vibrations, often tied to New Age or Eastern mysticism. They lead to dangerous trances and divert trust away from God's healing power and can lead to spiritual deception.

Spirit Guides / Angel Communication Instruction Books - Claiming to receive guidance from spirit beings apart from God is spiritually dangerous. The Bible warns against masquerading spirits who are actually demons (2 Corinthians 11:14-15), and we're instructed to seek God's wisdom directly through prayer and Scripture.

Wicca / Witchcraft / Sorcery / Spells / Incantations / Spellbooks - These practices directly violate Scripture's prohibitions against sorcery and witchcraft and warnings that sorcerers will be cast into the lake of fire for eternal torment. These practices are dangerous as they involve reliance on supernatural powers apart from God, leading to spiritual bondage.

Yoga Instructions - Though often presented as "just stretching" exercise, yoga is rooted in Hindu deity worship in which people contort their bodies to glorify one of the 330 million Hindu deities. Yoga means "yoke or bind" to the Hindu deity, Shiva or Brahman, and the practice often includes meditation or blasphemous chanting that contradict biblical worship. Christians are cautioned to avoid practices that invite spiritual compromise or align the body and mind with pagan concepts. So-called 'holy yoga' doesn't redeem yoga. Pilates that avoids all yoga asanas is recommended instead.

Authors to Avoid

It's just as important to get rid of new age and false gospel books, as it is to throw away other items of spiritual deception. If you have books in your home by any of these authors, please pray for God's discernment and strength as you go through your book collection.

Unfortunately, a lot of people who are newly saved out of the new age, start to follow authors who seem to be Christian because they quote the Bible or have a television show or podcast. Yet their books are littered with new age principles such as "law of attraction" name-it-and-claim-it prosperity teachings.

For example, I followed Joyce Meyer when I was first saved because she taught principles that seemed familiar while she held a Bible in her hands. Well, after studying the Bible further and researching through discernment ministries, I realized that her work seemed familiar because it was like the new age teachings that I'd just left! She was twisting Scripture and teaching a me-centered view of the Gospel. Please pray for her and her followers.

A lot of these authors' books on this list influenced the deception that I was under before God saved me. I used to tour and was friends with many of the authors on this list, and it breaks my heart to see that they're still ensnared in darkness. They don't talk to me anymore now that I'm a Christian who has renounced the new age. Please pray for God to save them out of darkness so that they'll renounce their old work.

Some of these authors may be your favorites, and their work may have helped you. So, if you're offended or surprised to see their names here, please pray for God's discernment and wisdom. You can find additional discernment research material about many of these authors on Christian discernment websites such as:

CHAPTER 7: NEW AGE AND FALSE GOSPEL BOOKS TO REMOVE FROM...

- Berean Research
- Christian Answers for the New Age
- Fighting for the Faith
- Good Fight Ministries
- Lighthouse Trails Research Project
- Michelle Lesley
- NAR Connections
- Servants of Grace

Several of the authors on this list appear to be Christian pastors, yet they teach an unbiblical "Christianized" version of the new age Law of Attraction called "Word of Faith" or "Name it and Claim it), instead of trusting in God's will and provision. They also emphasize materialism, covetousness, and acquiring wealth instead of focusing upon salvation and Bible study. This is one more reason why we need to read our Bibles and compare everything to Scripture so that we won't be deceived.

Please don't let the length of this list frustrate you. Once we study the Bible and develop a Biblical worldview, false teachings become immediately apparent. It's like someone who's able to detect musical notes that are off-pitch and out-of-tune because their ears are accustomed to hearing in-tune music.

Remember that the Bible condemns those who teach false prophecy or a false Gospel. Getting these materials out of your home is obedience to God:

> "And have no fellowship with the unfruitful works of darkness, but rather expose them." Ephesians 5:11

Authors with New Age, Occultic, or False Gospel Teachings to Remove from Your Home (alphabetized according their first names):

Alan Cohen (His writings promote New Age spirituality and metaphysical ideas that contradict biblical teachings on God, sin, and salvation.)

Alberto Villoldo (A former medical anthropologist and shamanic practitioner, Villoldo blends indigenous healing traditions with spiritual practices that may conflict with biblical teachings.)

Aleister Crowley (Known as "The Beast 666," Crowley was a prominent occultist and founder of Thelema, advocating for practices that are diametrically opposed to Christian doctrine.)

Alex Sanders (A British occultist and high priest in the Wiccan tradition, Sanders founded Alexandrian Wicca, promoting witchcraft and ceremonial magic incompatible with Christianity.)

Alexander Pagani (Known for unbiblical teachings on deliverance and spiritual warfare, often promoting sensationalism not grounded in Scripture.)

Alice Bailey (A leading figure in Theosophy, Bailey introduced esoteric teachings such as the "seven rays" and advocated for a new world religion, diverging from biblical Christianity.)

Anthony William (Known as the "Medical Medium," William claims to channel information from a spirit guide, offering health advice that lacks scientific validation and may lead individuals away from needed medical intervention.)

Anton LaVey (Founder of the Church of Satan, LaVey authored The Satanic Bible, promoting atheistic Satanism and occult rituals that are in direct opposition to Christian beliefs.)

CHAPTER 7: NEW AGE AND FALSE GOSPEL BOOKS TO REMOVE FROM...

Barbara Marciniak (An author and channeler, Marciniak claims to communicate with extraterrestrial beings known as the Pleiadians, promoting New Age philosophies that conflict with Christian teachings.)

Barbara Marx Hubbard (Hubbard proposed a vision of humanity's evolution into "co-creators" with God, blending New Age spirituality with a vision of human divinity that contradicts biblical teachings.)

Benny Hinn (Televangelist known for false gospel theatrical crusades and prosperity teaching.)

Beth McCord (Unbiblical Enneagram teacher which emphasizes personality and pridefulness and not the Gospel of Jesus Christ)

Beth Moore (While once respected in evangelical circles, she has been criticized for emotionalism, claiming to receive private messages from God that contradict Scripture, and an increasing drift toward ecumenism and progressive ideologies.)

Bill Johnson (a self-appointed "apostle" for Bethel Redding, which openly teaches new age beliefs and emphasizes signs and wonders over biblical doctrine.)

Brian Weiss (A psychiatrist who popularized past life regression therapy, Weiss promotes the belief in reincarnation and spiritual healing through regression, concepts not supported by Scripture.)

Brother Lawrence (His emphasis on mystical union with God can lead to a form of contemplative spirituality that lacks a strong scriptural foundation and can lead to deception with demons masquerading as the presence or voice of God, since contemplative practices lead to trances when the Bible warns us to stay alert and sober-minded to avoid the devil's schemes.)

Byron Katie (Creator of "The Work," Katie promotes a method of self-inquiry that is experiential and not Biblical. She teaches relativism instead of God's absolute truth.)

Carlos Castaneda (An anthropologist and author, Castaneda wrote about his experiences with shamanism and hallucinogenic substances, promoting practices that are incompatible with Christian teachings.)

Carol Bowman (Bowman writes stories of children supposedly remembering their past lives and includes anecdotes to "prove" that reincarnation is true such as children finding their former grave site. As Christians, we know that demons can masquerade and counterfeit, including leading people into the deception of "past life memories.")

Carolyn Myss (Myss integrates Jungian psychology and new age concepts like energy healing, clairvoyance and mindfulness, which may lead to beliefs outside of biblical Christianity.)

Catherine Ponder (A New Thought leader, Ponder promotes prosperity gospel teachings, encouraging financial contributions as a means to receive divine blessings, a concept not supported by Scripture.)

Charles Fillmore (Co-founder of the new thought Unity Church, Fillmore promoted teachings such as reincarnation and the divinity of humanity, which are not aligned with biblical Christianity.)

Christopher L. Heuertz (Author of The Sacred Enneagram — integrates unbiblical spirituality with Enneagram teachings)

CHAPTER 7: NEW AGE AND FALSE GOSPEL BOOKS TO REMOVE FROM...

Clarissa Pinkola Estés (Author of 'Women Who Run With the Wolves,' Estés explores the "wild woman" archetype through folklore and psychology, emphasizing feminine spirituality that conflicts with biblical teachings on gender and identity, and encouraging women to act out on their wild side which could include sinful indulgences.)

Colette Baron-Reid (Baron-Reid promotes clairvoyance, spirit guide, mediumship, oracle card readings and other divination practices that are incompatible with Christianity.)

Creflo Dollar (Unbiblical prosperity teachings and emphasis upon material acquisition instead of upon salvation and sanctification.)

Dallas Willard (Blends contemplative and philosophical mysticism, often promoting spiritual formation practices that can blur biblical discernment.)

Dan Millman (Millman blends Eastern philosophies with visions and self-help strategies, promoting new age teachings.)

Deepak Chopra (A prominent figure in New Age spirituality, Chopra integrates Eastern philosophies with Western medicine, promoting concepts like mind-body healing and the law of attraction that diverge from biblical teachings.)

Don Miguel Ruiz (Author of 'The Four Agreements,' Ruiz promotes Toltec wisdom and spiritual practices that conflict with Christian teachings.)

Dion Fortune (A British occultist and author, Fortune was a prominent figure in the Hermetic Order of the Golden Dawn, promoting esoteric occultic teachings that are incompatible with Christianity.)

Dolores Cannon (A hypnotherapist and author, Cannon developed the Quantum Healing Hypnosis Technique, promoting past life regression and contact with extraterrestrial beings, concepts not supported by Scripture.)

Doreen Valiente (A British Wiccan high priestess, Valiente authored several works on witchcraft and neopaganism, promoting practices that are incompatible with Christian teachings.)

Doreen Virtue (2017 or earlier books or cards) (Formerly a prominent figure in New Age spirituality, Virtue has since renounced her previous teachings and now promotes Christian-based content and her books published in 2025 or later are Biblical.)

Eckhart Tolle (Author of 'The Power of Now' and promoted by Oprah, Tolle teaches Eastern concepts as paths to spiritual awakening that are not compatible with biblical Christianity.)

Edgar Cayce (Known as the "sleeping prophet," Cayce provided psychic readings on topics like reincarnation and holistic health advice from mediumship with deceased physicians, promoting ideas that diverge from Christian doctrine.)

Eliphas Levi (A French occultist and author, Levi was a prominent figure in the development of modern occultism, promoting esoteric teachings that are incompatible with Christianity.)

Emmanuel Swedenborg (He claimed to have visions and personal conversations with angels and spirits, and he emphasized unbiblical and spiritually dangerous personal spiritual experiences.)

Emmet Fox (A New Thought minister, Fox promoted metaphysical interpretations of Christianity, encouraging practices like affirmations, manifesting, and visualization that conflict with Biblical Christian teachings.)

Ernest Holmes (Founder of the Religious Science new thought movement, Holmes promoted unbiblical teachings such as the divinity of humanity, mediumship in the first edition of his book, and the law of attraction.)

Esther Hicks "Abraham-Hicks" (Hicks channels a group of non-physical entities known as Abraham, promoting the law of attraction, that we humans are "gods," and other New Age concepts that diverge from biblical teachings.)

Evelyn C. Rysdyk (Rysdyk specializes in shamanic practices and indigenous healing traditions, promoting beliefs that conflict with Christian teachings.)

Florence Scovel Shinn (A New Thought author, Shinn promoted metaphysical and unbiblical practices like affirmations and visualization.)

Gary Zukav (Author of 'The Seat of the Soul,' Zukav promotes concepts like soul evolution and the law of attraction, ideas that diverge from biblical teachings.)

Gerald Gardner (A British occultist and author, Gardner founded Wicca and promoted witchcraft and neopaganism, practices that are incompatible with Christianity.)

Gordon Smith (A psychic medium and author, Smith promotes mediumship communication with the deceased and other practices that are not supported by Scripture.)

Hank Wesselman (An anthropologist and author, Wesselman promotes shamanic practices and beliefs in spirit worlds, ideas that diverge from biblical teachings.)

Helen Schucman (Channeler of the blasphemous and heretical 'A Course in Miracles,' Schucman channeled a demon masquerading as Jesus which taught messages that contradict the Bible.)

Helena Blavatsky (Co-founder of The Theosophical Society, Blavatsky promoted unbiblical esoteric teachings that were the root of modern new age beliefs, including mediumship, the occult, and teaching that Lucifer was a sympathetic character.)

Ian Morgan Cron (Co-author of 'The Road Back to You,' which promotes the me-centered and new age-rooted Enneagram.)

Ian Stevenson (A psychiatrist and author, Stevenson conducted research on past life memories, consciousness studies, dream visitations of deceased people, and promoted the belief in reincarnation and life after death, concepts not supported by Scripture.)

Isaiah Saldivar (Unbiblical deliverance and spiritual warfare teachings, often leading to theological errors and extra-biblical practices.)

J.Z. Knight (Claiming to channel an ancient entity named Ramtha, Knight promotes teachings that blend New Age spirituality with elements of mysticism and the occult.)

CHAPTER 7: NEW AGE AND FALSE GOSPEL BOOKS TO REMOVE FROM...

Jack Kornfield (A Buddhist teacher and author, Kornfield promotes mindfulness and meditation practices that are rooted in Eastern philosophies, beliefs which contradict biblical Christianity.)

James Redfield (Author of 'The Celestine Prophecy,' Redfield promotes new age concepts of spiritual awakening, esoteric visions, interpreting signs and omens, and synchronicity.)

James Van Praagh (A psychic medium and author, Van Praagh promotes mediumship communication with the deceased and other practices condemned by Scripture.)

Jane Roberts (Author of the Seth Material, Roberts claimed to channel an entity named Seth, promoting teachings that blend New Age spirituality with elements of mysticism and the occult.)

Jean Houston (An author and speaker, Houston promotes human potential and spiritual awakening, integrating New Age philosophies that conflict with Christian teachings.)

Joe Dispenza (Author of 'Breaking the Habit of Being Yourself,' Dispenza promotes the idea that individuals can change their reality through thought and meditation, concepts that diverge from biblical teachings.)

Joel Osteen (Popular megachurch pastor teaching new age-like law of attraction "name it and claim it" prosperity gospel with no discussion of the need for repentance of sins.)

John Edward (A psychic medium and author, Edward promotes necromancy communication with the deceased and other practices condemned by Scripture.)

John Randolph Price (A new age author who sprinkles in some twisted Bible verses, his books emphasize manifesting prosperity, spirit communication, and other dangerous practices).

Jon Kabat-Zinn (Pioneer of secular mindfulness rooted in Buddhist meditation practices, which encourages trances and observing thoughts without judgment that contradicts Biblical teachings about taking every thought captive and Jesus' Sermon on the Mount about sinful thoughts being equivalent to sinful actions.)

Joseph Murphy (A New Thought minister and author of The Power of Your Subconscious Mind, Murphy promoted metaphysical ideas that suggest the mind has divine creative power, which conflicts with the biblical truth of God's sovereignty.)

Joseph Prince (Singaporean pastor known for "grace and prosperity" teachings that downplay sin and emphasize health and acquiring wealth through your thoughts and words.)

Joyce Meyer (Televangelist and author who teaches the false prosperity gospel and unbiblical Word of Faith concepts.)

Kenneth Copeland (One of the most prominent Word of Faith false teachers, he advocates unbiblical "decree and declare" theology.)

Kris Vallotton (Vallotton claims to be a prophet who sees "power animals" and uses "bubbles of purple light for protection" and other new age concepts. Mark and avoid authors and books from Bethel Redding, which tries to blend new age teachings and practices with

CHAPTER 7: NEW AGE AND FALSE GOSPEL BOOKS TO REMOVE FROM...

Christianity.)

Krishnamurti (An Eastern philosopher, Krishnamurti taught self-realization and inward transformation, concepts that contradict the biblical view of truth and salvation.)

Lee Carroll (Channels an entity called "Kryon," offering teachings about ascension, energy shifts, and divine evolution, which are deeply rooted in New Age theology.)

Lisa William (A psychic medium who claims to communicate with the dead and angels which are practices that Scripture explicitly warns against.)

Louise L. Hay (Founder of Hay House Publishing and author of 'You Can Heal Your Life,' Hay taught that we control reality with our thoughts instead of acknowledging God's sovereignty. Her ideas were rooted in new thought and new age beliefs rather than Scripture.)

Lynn Andrews (Author of 'Medicine Woman' and other works on shamanism and feminine spirituality, Andrews blends Native American mysticism with esoteric practices that are incompatible with Christianity.)

Lysa TerKeurst (Her Proverbs 31 ministry originated through Steven Furtick's unbiblical teachings, and Lysa carries the same me-centered instead of Jesus-centered approach. She also partners with false teachers and teaches the unbiblical contemplative prayer method.)

Manly P. Hall (A mystic and Freemason, Hall wrote extensively on occult and esoteric philosophy, including 'The Secret Teachings of All

Ages,' which promotes Gnosticism, occultic symbolism, and spiritual practices condemned in Scripture.)

Marianne Williamson (Author of 'A Return to Love,' Williamson popularized 'A Course in Miracles' and teaches New Age ideas that use the name of Jesus in vain, and reframe sin, atonement, and salvation in non-biblical terms.)

Mary Baker Eddy (Founder of Christian Science and author of 'Science and Health with Key to the Scriptures,' Eddy blasphemously taught that Jesus was a created mortal man, denied the reality of illness and sin, and taught doctrines contrary to Christianity.)

Meister Eckhart (A medieval mystic whose pantheistic teachings blur the line between Creator and creation.)

Michael Harner (Anthropologist and founder of "core shamanism," Harner taught spiritual journeying and communication with spirits, which Scripture warns against.)

Michael Newton (A hypnotherapist who claimed to explore "life between lives" through past life regression, which are ideas rooted in reincarnation and incompatible with the Bible's view of the afterlife.)

Miguel Ruiz (Author of 'The Four Agreements,' he promotes Toltec beliefs and spiritual relativism, which are incompatible with Christianity.)

Napoleon Hill (Author of 'Think and Grow Rich,' Hill blended self-help with occult ideas, including conversations with "invisible counselors" and teachings about manifesting reality through thought.)

CHAPTER 7: NEW AGE AND FALSE GOSPEL BOOKS TO REMOVE FROM...

Neale Donald Walsch (Author of 'Conversations with God,' Walsch claimed to receive divine revelations that present a universalist and New Age view of God, contrary to the gospel of Jesus Christ.)

Norman Vincent Peale (Author of 'The Power of Positive Thinking,' Peale promoted man-centered ideas similar to New Thought, emphasizing mental attitude over sin, grace, and the gospel message.)

Oprah Winfrey (Promotes new age, occultic, Wicca, and witchcraft books and tarot cards on her website, and teaches a me-centered feministic and new age approach to life.)

Paulo Coelho (His novels, like 'The Alchemist,' convey occult themes, pantheism, and relativism that contradict the gospel of Christ.)

Paramahansa Yogananda (Founder of the Self-Realization Fellowship and author of 'Autobiography of a Yogi,' Yogananda promoted Eastern mysticism, meditation, and the divinization of the self.)

Pema Chödrön (A Buddhist nun and author, Chödrön teaches Eastern mindfulness and detachment based on Tibetan Buddhism, which contradicts the Christian worldview.)

Phineas Quimby (Considered the father of New Thought, Quimby was a hypnotist/mesmerizer who unbiblically taught that Jesus was merely a mortal role model to teach us that illness stems from wrong beliefs and that mental correction leads to healing. He influenced Mary Baker Eddy to start Christian Science.)

Radleigh Valentine (An astrologer and tarot card reader and former collaborator with Doreen Virtue, Valentine promotes angel tarot cards and other divination practices strictly prohibited in the Bible.)

Ram Dass / born Richard Alpert (Former Harvard professor turned Hindu spiritual teacher, Dass promoted Eastern meditation and reincarnation, which conflict with Christian teachings about salvation and the afterlife.)

Raven Grimassi (Author and teacher of Italian witchcraft (Strega) and Wicca, Grimassi promoted neopagan beliefs and magickal practices contrary to Scripture.)

Raymond Buckland (A major figure in modern Wicca and author of 'Buckland's Complete Book of Witchcraft,' he taught magical rituals and spirit communication, both of which are condemned in Scripture.)

Raymond Moody (Author of 'Life After Life,' Moody popularized near-death experiences and proposed theories about the afterlife that often align with New Age or universalist views.)

Rebecca Rosen (A psychic medium who claims to contact spirits of the dead and deliver spiritual messages - practices the Bible condemns as dangerous and forbidden.)

Rhonda Byrne (Author of 'The Secret,' Byrne teaches the Law of Attraction and borrows heavily from the trance-channeled Abraham-Hicks, which unbiblically claims that thoughts can control reality.)

Richard Bach (His books, such as 'Jonathan Livingston Seagull,' promote self-deification and metaphysical beliefs contrary to Christianity.)

Richard Dawkins (An outspoken atheist who actively mocks Christian-

CHAPTER 7: NEW AGE AND FALSE GOSPEL BOOKS TO REMOVE FROM...

ity and promotes naturalism as an alternative to faith in God.)

Richard Foster (Popularized unbiblical spiritual formation practices like contemplative prayer, which can lead people into trances and think they're receiving personal messages from God when they're not.)

Rick Warren (Has prosperity gospel and motivational speeches tendencies in his books, rather than focusing upon Gospel-centered Bible expository preaching. He also has ecumenical compromises in promoting the pope and Roman Catholicism instead of warning about the theological differences.)

Rosemary Altea (A spiritual healer and medium, Altea claims to communicate with spirits and angels, promoting beliefs outside of biblical teaching.)

Rudolf Steiner (Founder of Anthroposophy, Steiner taught reincarnation, karma, and occult science, leading to syncretistic teachings far from the gospel.)

Ruth Montgomery (A journalist turned channeler, Montgomery wrote books on reincarnation and guidance from spirit beings, introducing many readers to occultic ideas.)

Sanaya Roman (Channels spirit guides and promotes New Age ascension teachings, which are occult and spiritually dangerous.)

Scott Cunningham (Author of books on solitary witchcraft and Wicca, Cunningham's writings introduce readers to spells, rituals, and neopagan practices incompatible with Scripture.)

Shirley MacLaine (Actress and author who openly promotes reincarnation, channeling, and other New Age practices in books and movies like 'Out on a Limb.')

Silver RavenWolf (A prominent Wiccan author on witchcraft and spellcasting - dangerous content that directly contradicts biblical principles.)

Sonia Choquette (Choquette encourages divination, spirit guide communication, and other New Age practices that the Bible warns against.)

Sri Chinmoy (Spiritual teacher who combined Eastern meditation and philosophy, encouraging self-divinization and spiritual enlightenment without Christ.)

Starhawk (Feminist and Wiccan priestess, Starhawk promotes goddess worship and earth-centered spirituality, dangerous teachings that oppose biblical truth.)

Stephen Hawking (Atheist who denied the existence of God and promoted a materialist worldview.)

Steven Furtick (Often preaches motivational messages with questionable theology including the heresy of modalism, and portrays a man-centered gospel including inserting himself into Bible stories. His Elevation music should also be avoided.)

Stuart Wilde (New Age teacher and author who advocated affirmations, visualization, and metaphysical self-empowerment that put man, not God, at the center.)

CHAPTER 7: NEW AGE AND FALSE GOSPEL BOOKS TO REMOVE FROM...

Suzanne Stabile (Co-author of 'The Road Back to You,' which promotes the me-centered and new age-rooted Enneagram.)

Sybil Leek (One of the first popular British witches, Leek promoted astrology and the occult in mainstream media, encouraging beliefs the Bible explicitly forbids.)

Sylvia Browne (A psychic medium who claimed to speak with spirits and angels and who taught blasphemously about Jesus, Browne's books blend spiritual deception with messages incompatible with the Bible.)

T.D. Jakes (Megachurch pastor with prosperity teachings and a history of teaching modalism and an association with Oneness Pentecostalism.)

Theresa Caputo (Known as the "Long Island Medium," Caputo claims to communicate with the dead, practicing mediumship that Scripture strongly condemns.)

Thich Nhat Hanh (A Vietnamese Buddhist monk and author who promotes Eastern mindfulness and interspiritual dialogue.)

Thomas Keating (A proponent of contemplative practices rooted in Eastern mysticism rather than biblical meditation.)

Thomas Merton (A Trappist monk who merged mysticism with Eastern philosophies, leading to syncretism and theological confusion.)

Tyler Henry (A celebrity medium who claims to deliver messages from the dead - dangerous practices that directly contradict biblical commands against necromancy.)

Wayne Dyer (A self-help author who promoted new age and Eastern concepts of self-actualization, unbiblical teachings about Jesus, ecumenism, universalism, and divine selfhood.)

Publishers of New Age Books to Remove from Your Home

We also want to avoid owning books from these publishers which specialize in new age, new thought, and occultic books. Please pray for God to save the people who work for these publishers:

- Balboa Press
- Destiny Books
- Hay House
- Inner Traditions / Bear & Company
- Llewellyn Publications
- Moon Books
- Sounds True
- Theosophical Publishing House
- Watkins Publishing
- Weiser Books

How to Discern If a Book is Appropriate for Christians

As we've discussed, some books are obviously unbiblical such as witchcraft spell books. Yet, other books may appear to be Christian. How can you discern whether a book is appropriate for your Christian household?

Here are some guidelines to help you evaluate the books you have:

- *What is the source of the teaching?* Consider where the ideas in the book come from. Does the book promote biblical truth, or does it rely

CHAPTER 7: NEW AGE AND FALSE GOSPEL BOOKS TO REMOVE FROM...

upon worldly wisdom or spiritual teachings outside of Scripture? If a book draws from secular, Eastern, or New Age teachings, or promotes self-sufficiency, "attracting prosperity with your thoughts or words," or idolizing something apart from God, these are red flags.

• *Does this book align with biblical principles?* Evaluate the message of the book against Scripture. Does it teach that Jesus Christ is the only way to salvation (John 14:6)? Does it encourage trusting in the Lord, or does it suggest that you can shape your own reality apart from God's will? Does it promote communication with spirits, or trying to predict your future? Is it emphasizing using your thoughts, words, vision boards, or "decree and delare prayers" to gain material abundance? Does it twist Bible verses or stories out-of-context to try to justify its unbiblical teachings? Does it encourage you to be a "demon slayer" instead of praying for Jesus' intervention and protection? If the book contradicts biblical truths about God's sovereignty or the gospel, it's not appropriate for Christians.

• *What is the underlying* worldview? We want to stick with books that have a biblical worldview, which means seeing everything through the lens of God's will which we learn by studying the Bible. A secular worldview is the belief that people are in charge and must make things happen according to their own will ("follow your heart," "believe in yourself"), while a biblical worldview knows that God is sovereign and we want to follow His will. Does the book promote a Christian worldview that acknowledges God's authority over all things? Or does it promote a worldview that encourages personal empowerment? If it's putting humans at the center instead of God, it's best to toss the book.

• *Does it promote idolatry or spiritual deception?* Books that encourage you to seek answers from anything other than God (like crystals, astrology, dreams, cards, or the Law of Attraction) are often subtly drawing you into spiritual deception. If a book promotes practices that conflict with worshiping our one true God, it should be tossed.

What About Keeping New Age & Occultic Books for Research and Discernment Purposes?

If you're considering keeping some New Age books for the sake of research or to warn others about the contents of these teachings, prayerfully consider the effects of having these books in your home and of reading them as a Christian. These books are filled with false teachings and deceptive ideologies. The Bible warns us about exposing ourselves to harmful influences, even if our intention is to counter them:

> *"Do not be deceived: 'Bad company ruins good morals.'"* (1 Corinthians 15:33)

> *"See to it that no one takes you captive through hollow and deceptive philosophy, which depends on human tradition and the elemental spiritual forces of this world rather than on Christ."* (Colossians 2:8)

Researching deceptive philosophies can subtly expose your mind and heart to ideas that may lead to confusion or compromise in your faith. Once you have a biblical worldview, it can be upsetting and depressing to read false teachings. While your intention is to understand and teach others about these practices, the risk of spiritual contamination through continual exposure to New Age thought should not be underestimated.

Prolonged exposure to unbiblical ideologies could possibly cause subtle shifts in your worldview, erode your discernment, or desensitize you to the seriousness of these practices. What begins as intellectual engagement could develop into spiritual curiosity or influence. The mind is a battleground, and the enemy could use "research" to plant seeds of doubt or confusion.

It's best to remove *all* forms of deception from your home and office. We can do discernment research without having physical copies of false teachings in our homes.

"Above all else, guard your heart, for everything you do flows from it." (Proverbs 4:23)

Practical Steps for Removing Books

If you've identified books that are incompatible with Christianity, it's important to remove them from your home:

1. *Pray for discernment*: Ask God to help you evaluate your books with wisdom and to show you anything that might be leading you away from Him.

2. *Go through your bookshelves and boxes of books*: Review the books that you have, as you pray for the Holy Spirit to guide you in making decisions about what should stay and what should go. The Holy Spirit will convict you to remove books that contradict Jesus' teachings. If in doubt about a book, throw it out. Remember that the new Christians burned millions of dollars of sorcery materials in Acts 19:19.

3. *Remove anything that's unbiblical*: If you find books on astrology, witchcraft, divination, the Law of Attraction, "Christian" books that twist Scripture, or anything else that doesn't align with the truth of the gospel, it's time to let them go. **Please don't donate or sell books**

with false teachings, as we don't want to pass along the deception. Instead, dispose of them either in the garbage, or burn them, or pour oil or water over them, or shred them.

4. *Replace with Biblical truth*: Fill your home with books that increase your knowledge of God's Word, and encourage your faith, trust, and growth in your relationship with God. Purchase new or used Study Bibles that have commentaries next to Scripture as resources for daily reading. Look for Christian authors who write about biblically solid theology, and prioritize books that align with biblical truth. Warren Wiersbe's books are among my favorites.

As Christians, we must be careful about what we read, ensuring that the books we allow into our homes align with God's Word and help us grow in our relationship with Him. We also want to make sure that we only have books that stand upon biblical truth, in case our children or visitors are influenced by books they find in our home.

Checklist for Removing New Age Books from Your Home

On the next page, you'll see a room-by-room checklist to use as you go through your home to identify and discard any false teaching books. Be sure to look in your closets, boxes, bathroom, drawers, car, and other places where you may have placed books.

REMOVING NEW AGE FROM YOUR HOME

KITCHEN	LIVING ROOM
☐	☐
☐	☐
☐	☐
☐	☐
☐	☐
☐	☐
☐	

HALLWAY / ENTRY	BEDROOM
☐	☐
☐	☐
☐	☐
☐	☐
☐	☐
☐	☐
☐	

OTHER	BATHROOM
☐	☐
☐	☐
☐	☐
☐	☐
☐	☐
☐	☐
☐	

Chapter 8: Conjuring Tools of Wicca, Witchcraft, and the Occult

We've already discussed the need to get witchcraft, Wiccan, and occultic tools out of the home. This chapter will go into more detail for those who aren't familiar with the reason why these tools need to be removed from Christian homes.

Conjuring means trying to make something happen with your own power and strength. Witchcraft in particular is a based upon a desire for personal power, often derived through casting spells and invoking spirits (demons).

Many people who've gone through personal trauma have fears about trusting others, including God. Sadly, some trauma survivors turn to spell books or videos that teach them to rely upon their own power. The trouble is that witchcraft "borrows" their power from spirits that pretend to be helpful as a way of ingratiating people.

Those in the new age would probably be surprised to realize that they're also involved in witchcraft conjuring methods. Yet, any time we turn to an object to get something by invoking spirits; by speaking affirmations, decrees, or delarations; or by using our senses (such as visualizing), we're involved with conjuring just like witches.

Phrases like "manifest your dream life," "speak it into existence," "your thoughts control your reality" and "use your energy to attract abundance" are popular across social media and wellness platforms.

And in some Christian circles, similar attempts to conjure use phrases that may sound Biblical on the surface - like "I decree and declare" or "your words become your reality" - yet anyone who knows their Bible realizes that they're not.

As Christians, we're instructed to:

- Pray for God's help
- Trust in the Lord
- Wait upon the Lord's timing
- Lean upon God's strength and power
- Follow God's lead

Those who use conjuring tools and methods are often impatient with God's timing, or they haven't learned to trust Him. To conjure means "to call upon or command a spirit or force," or "to bring something into existence by supernatural means." When we use spiritual or symbolic tools to try and force our will to come to pass - especially without first seeking the Lord - we step outside of trust and obedience to God. We are essentially trying to become god over our own lives.

When we attempt to manifest outcomes, manipulate energy, or harness unseen forces to "make things happen," we're conducting sorcery - even if we're doing it under the label of "Christian manifestation" or "faith-based affirmations." We can't blend light with darkness (2 Corinthians 6:14-15). God will not share His glory with idols (Isaiah 42:8).

So, let's make sure that you don't have any of these conjuring tools in your home. This is not an exhaustive list, and you may find other items in your home related to this list. If you do, it's time to remove them:

Altar with Manifestation Tools - Decorated tables with candles, crystals, figurines, bowls used for setting up a space for ritual, prayer, visualizing, or magick. It's possible to clear the items off of the table, and

CHAPTER 8: CONJURING TOOLS OF WICCA, WITCHCRAFT, AND THE...

then keep the table; however, you'd need to pray for the Holy Spirit's leading on this. If the sight of the table triggers painful memories of your pre-salvation days, or if it tempts you to revert to your old rituals, it's best to remove the table from your home.

Athame (Ritual Knife) - A small double-edged dagger, often black-handled which isn't sharpened for physical cutting. It's used like a wand in Wicca and other occult practices which symbolizes the element of air or fire to channel the user's will or spiritual power.

Besom (Witch's Broom) – Small broom made of twigs or herbs used for witchcraft ceremonial "sweeping" of spiritual energy to cleanse and purify ritual spaces.

Crystal Balls Glass or crystal spheres, usually on a stand used for scrying, divination, or gazing to receive visions or insight.

Drumming Ceremony Equipment - Wooden hand-held leather-covered drum that's painted with spiritual symbols, and other equipment such as feather wands, used in full moon ceremonies where prayers are directed to the moon instead of to God who created the moon. Appropriated from Native American spirituality and utilized by new agers to "manifest" and "banish."

Essential Oils (Used as Idols Spiritually). Small bottles of oils labeled "third eye," "abundance," "protection," "clearing," "romance," etc. used for anointing, spellwork, meditation, and in the unbiblical belief that they provide spiritual protection instead of following God's Word to put on the Armor of God. The oils in the Bible are distilled, not essential oils and the Biblical oils were *never* used for personal manifesting. Using essential oils for fragrance, cleaning, health, and other non-idolatrous ways is spiritually neutral and not a problem. It's only a problem when essential oils are viewed as idols having their own powers apart from God, and the oils are glorified instead of God our Great Physician who protects and provides for us.

Incense & Burners (used for ceremonies and rituals). Sticks, cones, or loose incense with decorative holders. These holders are especially an issue if they have occultic symbols on them. Incense used for fragrance is spiritually neutral and not a problem. However, if the incense is viewed as an idol with a power apart from God, that's a problem.

Moon Water - Water stored in glass bottles or jars that was left outside under full moonlight. Believed to carry the moon's energy for use in spiritual cleansing, rituals, or "charging" objects.

Ouija Board / Spirit Board - Flat board printed with letters, numbers, and a pointer (planchette) used for divination and dangerous seances and spirit communication.

Ritual Candles (Colored or Anointed) – Short wide colored candles, sometimes labeled with intentions (e.g., "Love," "Money") used for manifesting, spells, focus, and energy attraction.

Ritual Clothing - We discussed in Chapter 5 the importance of getting ceremonial and ritual attire (such as capes, hoods, aprons, bags, etc.) out of your Christian home.

Runes / Rune Stones - Small stones or tiles engraved with symbols used for divination.

Sage Bundles / Smudge Sticks - Bundled dried herbs, especially white sage or palo santo appropriated from Native American and other indigenous cultures. When the bundles are lit on fire the smoke supposedly cleanses spaces, people, and objects of "negative energy."

Scrying Mirrors / Black Mirrors - Polished black mirrors, often circular used for "scrying" (seeing visions or spirits), divination, and communicating with spirits.

Spell Journals / Grimoires / Books of Shadows - Decorative or leather-bound notebooks filled with rituals, spells, dreams, journaling ceremonial experiences, and used as a personal occultic manual.

Vision Boards / Manifestation Boards - Poster boards with pictures and words that represent the person's goals and dreams. People are taught to look at this board and visualize that the images have already come true in the person's life. They're taught to use "positive affirmations," pagan new age prayers, and focused energy to attract these goals into existence. This is no different than the sorcery that witches use. There are no visualizations or vision boards in the Bible (despite what some professing Christians try to twist Habbukuk 2:2 to say).

These items and rituals invite dangerous demonic deception. They have no place in a Christian's life or in their home. They lead to idolatry where instead of trusting in God's provision, we place our faith in the items and rituals themselves as though they hold power to manipulate or alter our circumstances. As Christians, we're not called to use substances or practices to manifest our desires, but to seek God's will in all things (Matthew 6:33).

God is the one who provides for our needs, and He would never contradict Himself by requiring the rituals and objects which He condemns to bring about His will. In James 1:17, we're reminded that every good and perfect gift comes from God, not from conjuring tools or rituals. We must rely on Him to meet our needs.

Let us keep our eyes fixed on Christ. He is the source of all healing, wisdom, and peace, and let us avoid practices that could draw us into spiritual deception, sorcery, or idolatry.

Checklist for Removing Conjuring Items from Your Home

Here's a checklist to use, if you'd like, when walking through your home to find and remove false teaching books. Be sure to check your garage, closets, drawers, boxes, bathrooms, attic, basement, and even outdoor spaces.

CHECKLIST FOR REMOVING CONJURING ITEMS FROM YOUR HOME

KITCHEN	LIVING ROOM
☐	☐
☐	☐
☐	☐
☐	☐
☐	☐
☐	☐
☐	☐
☐	

HALLWAY / ENTRY	BEDROOM
☐	☐
☐	☐
☐	☐
☐	☐
☐	☐
☐	☐
☐	

OTHER	BATHROOM
☐	☐
☐	☐
☐	☐
☐	☐
☐	☐
☐	☐
☐	☐

Chapter 9: Deleting Digital New Age Items

Now that we've tackled the physical objects to remove from your home, let's look at the digital items which may be infiltrating new age or occult influences into your home through your phone, television, or other electronic devices.

New Age and occultic elements are often embedded into digital content, so we must be vigilant and discerning. These digital items, whether they're apps, music, or videos, can try to point us away from God's truth and potentially lead to deception and spiritual warfare.

Let's take a closer look at these digital items that we need to delete from our devices. This isn't an exhaustive list, so please use this list as a jumping-off point as you delete new age or occult apps from your devices:

New Age Music

We need to insure that the music to which we listen, sing, and play glorifies God. We are exhorted that, "whatever you do, do all to the glory of God" (1 Corinthians 10:31).

Music influences emotions, thoughts, and even theology. The Arianism heresy that falsely taught Jesus was a created being, was popularized through musical jingles which promoted Arianism during the time of Athanasius in the fourth century. So, music can popularize

CHAPTER 9: DELETING DIGITAL NEW AGE ITEMS

false teachings, which is one more reason why we must be discerning with our musical decisions.

New Age music is often used for meditation, relaxation, massage, and energy healing, and while it may seem harmless, there are several reasons why it doesn't belong in a Christian's life.

New Age music often includes sounds such as brass Tibetan bells and monotonous repetitious musical notes with reverb echo, designed to alter your consciousness. This can seem soothing, but heads up because New Age music is designed to induce a spiritual experience or an altered state of consciousness.

Often, this music is tied to practices such as guided visualization meditation where the goal is to seek answers through spirit guide communication. My husband played new age meditation music on his keyboard at my new age seminars, prior to our salvation in 2017. As he played this music, you could see the audience members' heads start to drop into ultra-relaxed positions. Looking back, we both regret how his music made them vulnerable to opening up to the new age deception that I unfortunately taught back then. We're grateful that he never recorded a music album.

The Bible warns us to be alert and sober-minded because the devil prowls around like a roaring lion seeking someone to devour (1 Peter 5:8). Relaxing is fine, but we don't want to be in trances such as new age music induces. If you get a massage, it's best to bring along your own set-list of worship music since most massage therapists use new age music during their sessions.

As you check your music apps for new age music to delete, also prayerfully check your collections of physical music items such as CD's and albums. I also got rid of my acoustic guitar that had new age symbols embossed onto it.

New Age Musicians

REMOVING NEW AGE FROM YOUR HOME

Here are some of the more famous new age musicians who have popular music albums, listed alphabetically by first name. I toured with many of them while giving new age workshops, and I ask that you please pray for God to save them out of new age deception. Please prayerfully go through your physical and digital music libraries and delete the music from these and similar musicians:

Andreas Vollenweider – Swiss harpist known for blending harp with global and ambient sounds.

Deuter – German instrumentalist known for meditation music combining Eastern and Western influences

Iasos - Considered to be a pioneer of new age music, he blended trance-inducing ethereal synthesizer sounds with whale and dolphin calls.

Llewellyn – UK-based composer known for Reiki, healing, and relaxation music.

Loreena McKennitt – Canadian artist fusing Celtic, Middle Eastern, and folk traditions with lyrics that often glorify paganism.

Lisa Gerrard – Vocalist from Dead Can Dance, blending world, ambient, and spiritual tones.

Paul Horn – Jazz flutist turned New Age pioneer, known for recording in "sacred spaces."

Peter Kater – Grammy-winning pianist and composer of emotive new age meditative music.

CHAPTER 9: DELETING DIGITAL NEW AGE ITEMS

Secret Garden (Rolf Løvland & Fionnuala Sherry) – Known for Celtic-infused orchestral New Age. I personally used their music for some of the meditations that led to my new age insights and writings so I consider their music to be especially spiritually dangerous.

Snatum Kaur - An American new age singer rooted in Sikh tradition.

Steven Halpern – Considered to be a pioneer of New Age music, often using brainwave entrainment. He was a friend of mine in the new age, and I pray for his salvation.

Suzanne Ciani – Electronic music pioneer, blending synthesizers with ambient tones.

Other Musical Influences

In addition to the genre of new age music, our theology, worldview, and spiritual safety could be affected by secular music. Musicians use their music to promote their worldviews. So, it's important to prayerfully look at our collection of music on our apps and our physical collections of CD's and albums.

I conducted three interviews about the effects of music for my YouTube.com/@Doreen_Virtue channel. Two interviews were with born-again young men who said they'd previously listened to AC/DC, which led them to Slayer and death metal music, where they got involved in occultism and satanism. Praise the Lord for saving them out of darkness! Now they warn people about the harmful effects of metal music.

The other interview with Pastor Joe Schimmel of Good Fight Ministries explained the occultic basis of Led Zeppelin and other heavy metal and rock bands. I used to listen to and play Led Zeppelin music before I was saved, and the interview with Pastor Joe explained about the satanic indoctrination of that music. Good Fight Ministries has a highly-recommended online documentary called, "They Sold Their Soul for Rock and Roll."

I can see now that my involvement in rock music as a listener and a musician influenced my worldview, false beliefs, and false teachings. This music is satanic, and it promotes doing whatever you want, which is the credo of satanism. Pastor Joe even showed how the Led Zeppelin 4 record album has the Satanic motto, "Do what thou wilt" and "so mote it be" embossed into the edges of the album! Well, I used to own and listen to that record album. It explains so much, so now we're warning others who have ears to hear. Many of the lyrics of popular rock music came to the lyricist through automatic channeling, which is mediumship that is condemned in the Bible.

Rock and metal musicians are often involved in new age or satanic practices, and their music reflects this. Before I was saved, I met many popular musicians backstage at my new age events. Several of them came to me for private psychic readings.

The musicians in particular who were part of my new age deception included Stevie Nicks and Led Zeppelin. I've played musical instruments since childhood when I took violin lessons. In adolescence I switched to playing guitar largely because of the influence of popular rock music. I have videos on my YouTube channel showing the witchcraft influences with Taylor Swift, also. I realize that these are beloved singers to some people. If you're offended, please pray for God's wisdom and do some research about these influences.

How can we insure that the music to which we listen, sing, and play, glorifies God?

1. Choose music with lyrics that are Bible verses.

CHAPTER 9: DELETING DIGITAL NEW AGE ITEMS

2. Know your Bible, so you can compare the lyrics of music to Scripture.
3. Notice whether your thoughts, emotions, and movements are God-honoring, as you listen to the music.
4. Avoid lyrics which are self-glorifying, elevating yourself instead of God.
5. Avoid lyrics which paint a false picture of Christ, such as romantically portraying Jesus as a boyfriend instead of as our Lord and Savior.
6. Avoid lyrics which glorify sinning.
7. Avoid music from unbiblical sources such as Jehovah Witness, Mormonism, eastern mysticism, new age, Christian Science, Bethel Redding, Hillsong, and Elevation, or any musician who endorses these false teachings.
8. Pray for God's wisdom in your musical selections.
9. Consult the discernment videos of Good Fight Ministries to learn more about specific musicians.
10. Remember that if a song is widely popular in the world, then it's probably singing about worldly beliefs instead of biblical truth.
11. Stick with classic hymns, or listen to The Getty's; Sovereign Grace Music; Nathan George Clark; Michael O'Brien and Scripture Lullabies.

Binaural Beats and Their Dangers

Binaural beats are another form of New Age music that often accompanies meditation or spiritual healing practices. The concept behind binaural beats is that listening to certain frequencies can help align the brain's alpha waves (the brain's natural state) to certain states of consciousness. While marketed as a way to reduce stress, improve focus, or achieve deeper meditation, the practice comes with occultic roots.

Some New Age teachings promote binaural beats as a tool to open up spiritual gateways to higher consciousness or even connect with the universal energy. Yet, the truth is that binaural beats lead to spiritually dangerous trances which the devil will exploit. The Bible exhorts us to remain alert and sober-minded (1 Peter 5:8). We can relax without going into a trance.

Philippians 4:8 tells us to focus on whatever is pure, lovely, and praiseworthy. While it's not wrong to use music for relaxation, we should be cautious about music or beats that encourage us to engage with spiritual forces outside of God's will. Music that promotes altered states of consciousness or connects us with demons is spiritually dangerous.

So, we will want to delete binaural beats apps from our devices and discard any headphones equipment that have built-in repetitive trance-inducing sounds.

Astrology Apps

Make sure to delete astrology or horoscope apps or programs from your devices. The Bible is clear in Deuteronomy 4:19 and Isaiah 47:13-14 that seeking guidance from the stars or any form of astrology is idolatry and spiritual rebellion against God. The Magi were *not* astrologers! Astrology leads people to believe in forces beyond God's control, often looking to the stars and planets for answers instead of trusting the Creator of those stars and planets. Many of these apps have links to websites that offer paid astrological charts.

Instead of relying upon astrology or horoscopes for guidance, we're called to seek God's wisdom through prayer, His Word, and the counsel of the Holy Spirit (James 1:5). When we trust in astrology, we place our faith in something other than God's Word, which can invite spiritual confusion, deception, and distraction.

Divination / Card Reading / Rune Reading / Numerology apps

We also want to delete apps that focus upon divination (seeking advice or knowledge of the future through paranormal means) include those that offer tarot readings, angel card readings, numerology readings, rune readings, IChing readings, palmistry, or other forms of the condemned practice of fortune-telling.

These apps claim to give insight into the future, relationships, or important life decisions by tapping into paranormal powers or energies associated with occultic or witchcraft practices. Many of these apps have links to websites that offer paid psychic readings.

The Bible clearly condemns divination and fortune-telling. Deuteronomy 18:10-12 states that the people who practices divination or sorcery are an abomination to God. These practices invoke demonic influences and create a dangerous reliance on anything other than God's wisdom and sovereignty.

Manifestation and Law of Attraction Apps

These apps need to be deleted from the devices of Christians because they teach and encourage sorcery conjuring through visualization, praying to the universe, virtual vision boards, affirmations, speaking your wishes into existence, or decreeing and declaring.

The core belief behind manifestation and the Law of Attraction is based on the condemned practices of sorcery and witchcraft. These are forms of conjuring that contradict the biblical principle that God is sovereign and in control of our lives.

Matthew 6:25-34 reminds us that we should seek first God's Kingdom and His righteousness, trusting Him to provide for our needs. The Law of Attraction and the "Christianized" decree and declare movement teach that humans have the power to control their destiny through their words, commands, visualizations, and thoughts, but this attempts to remove God's will from the equation. It's a product of the "follow your dreams" teachings which promote the worship of self and self-reliance, rather than complete dependence on God.

As Christians, we must trust in God's will and timing, and not try to manipulate spirits (demons) to fulfill our desires. Proverbs 3:5 exhorts us to trust in the Lord with all of our heart and not to lean upon our own understanding.

Energy Healing Apps

Some apps promote the use of crystal therapy, chakra balancing, and energy healing practices such as Reiki, claiming to help align our energy, heal emotional wounds, or even bring peace into our lives.

The Bible makes it clear that only God holds the power to heal, and we shouldn't turn to objects such as His creations, or practices outside of Him for our well-being (Exodus 15:26, Psalm 103:3). Using crystals or energy healing like Reiki can subtly lead us into idolatry or sorcery instead of placing our trust in God.

I was a Reiki master and certified Pranic energy healer, prior to God saving me. Reiki was invented by Mikao Usui who was a Buddhist spiritualist, even though one of his students fabricated a story that he was a Christian seminary professor to make Reiki more appealing to Westerners. Reiki and other energy healing is co-mingling with the unclean spirits that the Bible warns about. Instead of relying upon crystals or energy healing apps, we should seek God's wisdom and will through prayers for healing (James 5:14-15).

Meditation Apps

CHAPTER 9: DELETING DIGITAL NEW AGE ITEMS

The Bible discusses meditation as the very specific practice of focusing upon Scripture and reading it aloud. This is different than new age and Eastern forms of meditation that plant guided imagery into the mind, or ask you to notice your thoughts without judgment when the Bible tells us to take every thought captive and that sinful thoughts are the equivalent of sinful actions.

I regrettably led audiences in new age meditations and recorded new age meditation audios before God opened my eyes and saved me in 2017.

Now there are "Christian" Meditation Apps that are almost as bad as the new age meditation apps. These so-called Christian meditation apps guide people to engage in mystical practices such as Lectio Divina that arose out of the mystical monastic movement. It's not Biblical because it guides people to go into an altered state and to seek meanings about Scripture in supernatural ways, instead of asking a pastor or reading a reliable commentary or Study Bible. People using Lectio Divina imagine that God is explaining the true meaning of Scripture, in ways that are either their imagination or even demonic deception.

The "Christian" meditation apps also have troubling components such as new age music, contemplative practices such as the unbiblical "centering prayer," and breathwork that leads to altered states of consciousness.

Some of these apps also blasphemously guide people to pray to Mother Mary or Roman Catholic saints, when the Bible is clear that Jesus is our only mediator between humanity and Father God (1 Timothy 2:5). We don't turn to deceased humans as intercessors for our prayers.

For all of these reasons, please delete any meditation apps from your devices. If you need to relax, use an app to listen to the Bible such as the free ESV Bible app which has an audio feature with an optional timer that allows you to listen to Scripture as you relax or fall asleep.

Witchcraft & Wicca Apps

People turn to Wicca and witchcraft for personal power, and because they don't know or trust God and His timing and will. They instead turn to do-it-yourself methods of trying to make things happen according to their own will. The trouble is that it's dangerous to be outside of God's will by engaging in condemned practices such as witchcraft and sorcery which involve demonic deception.

These apps teach about spell casting, moon phase magick, potion recipes, and have ritual guides. These dangerous components point people away from Jesus and Bible study, and toward demons and self-glory.

There's no valid reason for a Christian to have this type of app upon his or her devices, and they need to be deleted right away with repentance.

Aura Reading Apps

This app works with the phone's camera to take a photo of someone with a supposed color of their aura outlining their head and shoulders. The app then offers an interpretation of what this aura color supposedly means.

This is divination and it's not based upon Biblical or scientific knowledge. Before I was saved, I used an aura reading app and found them to be inconsistent based upon what background colors were behind the person I photographed. So, in addition to being the condemned practice of divination, the app isn't even reliable. Time to delete this app and open our Bibles instead.

Spirit Communication Apps

CHAPTER 9: DELETING DIGITAL NEW AGE ITEMS

This type of app teaches and encourages mediumship, spirit guide communication, getting answers from virtual ouija boards, and channeling unclean spirits (demons). The app is usually linked to a website where paid readings are offered.

There's not one reason why a Christian would want to have this app on his or her devices. If you have an app like this, perhaps from your pre-salvation days, be sure to delete it.

Occult & Esoteric Teachings

These apps offer instruction in metaphysical topics and practices such as alchemy, Hermeticism, Theosophy, or "sacred geometry." I was involved in researching these topics before I was saved, in my pre-salvation quest for "hidden secrets" just like the lie that the serpent told Eve in the Garden. None of these teachings lead to anywhere but to more questions and deception. They're a waste of time and money at best, and an entry point to demonic deception and eternal torment at worst. Please delete apps like this.

Lucid dreams / Dream Interpretation / Astral Projection Apps

These apps encourage visualization practices, guided astral travel, out of body experiences, and other spiritually dangerous experiences. They usually offer dream interpretation with a mystical or occultic framework, and a link to get paid dream interpretations.

Spirit Animal / Power Animal / Shamanic Journeying Apps

These apps promise to help you gain answers and learn more about your personality and life purpose by finding your "power animal" through an online Shamanic journey. This is new age idolatry that appropriates from indigenous cultures.

Prior to salvation, I went through in-person Shamanic rituals such as sweat lodges, journeying, and drumming rituals to find my power animal - and these practices didn't yield the answers that I sought. Only through Jesus and Bible study did I find what I was seeking. If you have any Shamanic apps, please delete them.

Occult-Based Video Games & Simulations

Many video games have dark and occultic themes, which is why some Christians like the "Missionary Gamer ministry" in Idaho evangelize and share the Gospel within video games with other users. The trouble is that these video games have normalized witchcraft, sorcery, and the occult.

Apps now offer simulations where people can pretend they're witches casting spells. These apps involve dark magick and symbols from the occult. Please avoid and delete these apps, and keep your children away from them too.

News Apps with an Unbiblical Worldview

Everyone has a worldview, and many news agencies hold a worldview that excuses or promotes sins such as abortions or an unbiblical approach to relationships and marriage. Be sure that you're getting your news from sources which respect God's Word, and delete any app that pushes unbiblical propaganda.

New Age and Occultic Themed Movies

Many movies glorify the practices and things that God condemns, such as sorcery, witchcraft, adultery, lying, stealing, cursing, homosexuality,

CHAPTER 9: DELETING DIGITAL NEW AGE ITEMS

drunkenness, rewriting God's design for marriage, and so forth. It's actually tough to find a movie that doesn't go off of the biblical rails.

Even the so-called Christian movies include "follow your heart" messages, and Biblical portrayals take disturbing liberties with how they show our Lord and Savior Jesus speaking and acting.

So, do we need to avoid watching movies then? Well, we definitely need to be discerning. Movies by Rich and Dave Christiano are generally Gospel-centered in their themes, and many family-friendly movies are "safe" to watch. There are also some movies that are word-for-word portrayals from the Bible, that don't veer into changing Scripture.

Prior to watching a movie, read the summary, reviews, and YouTube comments about the movie. Christians are great at warning one another about unsuitable movies. Then, if you're watching a movie and a sin is glorified, stop the movie. If someone else is watching the movie with you, have a discussion about why that scene is unbiblical. Compare everything to Scripture.

In the meantime, be sure to delete or throw away any movies that blatantly glorify condemned sins. These movies are propaganda designed to normalize sin, and point people to sinful lifestyles instead of submission to God.

Discernment is Key

As Christians, we must carefully evaluate all of the digital content with which we engage. Purging digital New Age and occultic items is a way of being intentional about what we allow into our lives and our home. Be sure to check the apps on your childrens' devices, and delete any new age or occultic apps. I was too lenient with my kids' choices of video games and I regret this now.

By making a conscious decision to remove these items from our devices and lives, we help to protect ourselves from demonic deception and reaffirm our commitment to living according to God's Word.

Chapter 10: Bible Verses to Encourage You

Here are some Bible passages that encourage you to avoid false idols and to keep your home for the glory of God:

Exodus 20:3-5 – The First Commandment

"You shall have no other gods before me. You shall not make for yourselves an idol, or any likeness of anything that is in heaven above or on the earth below or in the waters beneath the earth. You shall not bow down to them or worship them."

- This commandment is still for today, and it encapsulates Jesus' summary of the "royal commandments" to love God. Loving God means obeying Him. God commands that no idols or false gods be worshiped, and this extends to the home. Creating or allowing idols to occupy one's home would violate this commandment, as it distracts from the true worship of God.

2. Joshua 24:14-15 (truncated) – Choose Whom You Will Serve

"Now therefore fear the Lord and serve him in sincerity and in faithfulness. Put away the gods that your fathers served beyond the River and in Egypt, and serve the Lord. And if it is evil in your

eyes to serve the Lord, choose this day whom you will serve . . . But as for me and my house, we will serve the Lord."

- Joshua, like Moses before him, called the Israelites to forsake any false gods or idols that may have been present in their homes. The choice to serve God must be made deliberately, and Joshua made it clear that his house would glorify God, leaving no room for idols. This is a strong message for Christians to forsake any idols that are taking Jesus' place upon their hearts - not just statues as idols, but anything that's elevated or obsessed about.

2 Kings 23:24-25 – Josiah Destroys Idols in the Land

> *"Moreover, Josiah put away the mediums and the necromancers and the household gods and the idols and all the abominations that were seen in the land of Judah and in Jerusalem, that he might establish the words of the law that were written in the book that Hilkiah the priest found in the house of the Lord. Before him there was no king like him, who turned to the Lord with all his heart and with all his soul and with all his might, according to all the law of Moses, nor did any like him arise after him."*

- King Josiah was praised for his dedication to God, which included removing all idols, false gods, and pagan practices from the land, including from people's homes. This passage stresses the importance of keeping your surroundings free of idols and staying loyal our one true God.

1 Corinthians 10:14 – Flee from Idolatry

CHAPTER 10: BIBLE VERSES TO ENCOURAGE YOU

"Therefore, my beloved, flee from idolatry."

- This verse warns Christians to avoid any type of idol, and to reject idolatry in all its forms. This includes anything in your home that could become an object of worship or devotion in place of God.

Deuteronomy 7:25-26 – The Destruction of Idols

"The carved images of their gods you shall burn with fire. You shall not covet the silver or the gold that is on them or take it for yourselves, lest you be ensnared by it, for it is an abomination to the Lord your God. And you shall not bring an abomination into your house and become devoted to destruction like it. You shall utterly detest and abhor it, for it is devoted to destruction."

- God spoke through Moses to instruct the Israelites to destroy idols in their home, since these objects would be a direct affront to God. This reinforces the Biblical teaching to keep our homes free of idols.

Romans 12:1-2 – Offering Your Life as a Living Sacrifice

"I appeal to you therefore, brothers, by the mercies of God, to present your bodies as a living sacrifice, holy and acceptable to God, which is your spiritual worship. Do not be conformed to this world, but be transformed by the renewal of your mind, that by testing you may discern what is the will of God, what is good and acceptable and perfect."

- While this passage isn't specifically about idols in the home, it emphasizes a life devoted to God. Our homes should reflect that we have offered our lives to God, and that we're not conforming to worldly practices or idols.

Isaiah 42:8 – God Will Not Share His Glory

"I am the Lord; that is my name; my glory I give to no other, nor my praise to carved idols."

- God declares that His glory can't be shared with idols. This underscores the seriousness of avoiding *any* form of idolatry, including in the home where we are to honor God with our lives.

Acts 17:29 – Idols Are Not Divine

"Being then God's offspring, we ought not to think that the divine being is like gold or silver or stone, an image formed by the art and imagination of man."

- Idols are made by human hands, and they have no place in a Christian's life or home.

Psalm 115:4-8 – The Foolishness of Idolatry

"Their idols are silver and gold, the work of human hands. They have mouths, but do not speak; eyes, but do not see; they have ears, but do not hear; noses, but do not smell; they have hands, but do not feel; feet, but do not walk; and they do not make a sound in their throat. Those who make them become like them; so do all who trust in them."

- Idols are powerless and meaningless, and those who trust in them become like them. A home filled with idols reflects a life of someone who doesn't know God, and this passage shows the foolishness of turning to idols instead of to God.

The Bible repeatedly emphasizes the importance of keeping one's home free from idols and to instead be dedicated to the worship of our one true God. Whether through commandments, exhortations, warnings, or examples, Scripture teaches that Christians and their homes should be sanctified and set apart for God's glory.

Chapter 11: As for Me and My House, We will Serve the Lord

Joshua proclaimed in Joshua 24:14-15 that he wouldn't have idols in his home but would instead dedicate his home to serving God. As Christians, we're called to do the same. Our purpose is to glorify God in *everything* that we do, without exception.

Jesus said that if we love Him, we must obey His commandments which He summarized as "love God and love our neighbors" (c.f., John 14:15). Loving God means to trust and obey Him.

We're saved by God's grace, and not by our works. Once we're saved and the Holy Spirit indwells us and we're given a new fleshly heart, we desire to please and obey God. Clearing idols out of our home is obedience. Obedience is evidence of our salvation.

God's grace doesn't give anyone a license to sin. We mustn't try to exploit God's grace by violating His commandments against paganism, idolatry, the occult, witchcraft, and sorcery. God's love means that He's willing to discipline us when we stray. The Holy Spirit convicts us in order to lead us to repentance and to the narrow path of obedience. The fruit of being indwelled by Holy Spirit include true and lasting peace and joy.

When we're saved out of new age or occultic deception, we must consider that Jesus died for those sins. Many of us were hell-bound, but God in His mercy and grace opened our eyes and saved us! Why would we want to keep any "trophies" from our pre-salvation days

Those items may have been expensive, yet we still need to destroy or discard them as the new Christians did when they publicly burned their expensive sorcery tools as recorded in Acts 19:19. They may have been sentimental gifts or heirlooms, yet our loyalty is to God (c.f., Galatians 1:10).

Don't Look Back

When God saved Lot and his family out of Sodom and Gomorrah, Lot's wife made the mistake of looking back even though she was warned not to do so. Because of her disobedience, she was instantly turned into a pillar of salt. Some theologians believe that she turned back because she longed for her old life and was reluctant to leave the sinful place.

Lot's wife didn't appreciate how God had given her an opportunity for redemption! We need to make sure that we appreciate that Jesus suffered and died for our sins, and that we've been given a new life in Christ. Jesus warned us to "Remember Lot's wife" as a warning not to cling to the world instead of trusting and obeying God (Luke 17:32).

Removing new age and occult items from your home is your way of *looking forward* to the new life which God has graciously given to you. We need to cut ties with our old life and remove any artifacts of who we were before Christ saved us.

The benefits of a Christian purging their home of New Age and occultic items are significant:

1. *Strengthened Relationship with God*

When we allow items tied to New Age or occultic practices into our homes, we invite spiritual confusion or distraction. These items represent beliefs and practices that God condemns in His Word.

Purging them removes temptations to regress back into occultic practices, and helps you to focus upon your relationship with God and serving Him. Keeping our homes free from false teachings and idols enables deeper fellowship with Him.

> *"But if we walk in the light, as he is in the light, we have fellowship with one another, and the blood of Jesus his Son cleanses us from all sin."* (1 John 1:7)

2. Freedom from Spiritual Bondage

Many New Age and occultic items invite demon as participants through invocations, divination, spell casting, idolatry, and spirit communication which results in spiritual oppression or bondage. By removing these items, you're physically severing any former partnership with demons that occurred during new age and occultic practices.

We will still have spiritual warfare as Christians. However, by removing object related to our previous dealings with demons, we won't be in the indentured servitude bondage that people in the new age and occult experience, especially those who earn an income through condemned new age and occultic practices such as being a professional psychic or energy healer.

> *"So if the Son sets you free, you will be free indeed."* (John 8:36)

3. Clarity and Peace of Mind

God is not the author of confusion - the devil is (c.f., 1 Corinthians 14:33). My home in the new age was crammed with divination tools, occultic books, and statues of idols. When we removed these items from our home, there was a palpable sense of peace in our home. Many people have told me of similar experiences of calmness after removing new age paraphernalia.

When our living spaces are filled with objects tied to false teachings or pagan rituals, they can create a sense of unease or confusion, even if we're unaware of it. Some people say that these items are possessed by demons, but there's no Biblical basis for that claim. Nor is there anything in the Bible that says these items "give demons legal rights."

Rather, the Bible says that bringing idolatrous objects into the home leads to defilement and judgment. These objects are an abomination to God, as are the people who use them (Deuteronomy 18:12).

4. **Witness to Others**

Removing New Age and occultic items from your home, and replacing them with items that honor God such as wall art with Bible verses, is a way of witnessing to those who live in or visit your home. Filling your home with God-honoring items demonstrates your commitment to serving God alone and can inspire others to do the same.

> "In the same way, let your light shine before others, that they may see your good deeds and glorify your Father in heaven." (Matthew 5:16)

This act of purging your home of idolatry and condemned practices isn't legalism, but rather a reflection of your desire to please and obey God. It's gratitude in action for His saving grace in your life.

All glory to God!

About the Author

Doreen Virtue holds a Master's degree in Biblical & Theological Studies with highest honors from Western Seminary (56 units / 2021), and an MA in Counseling Psychology from Chapman University. Prior to being saved by God's grace and mercy in 2017, Doreen was a psychotherapist specializing in women's issues, rated in the top 15 most influential living spiritual teachers by Watkins, and the top selling new age author in the world. She was born and raised in new thought churches which she attended for 33 years, before segueing to new age and Wicca in 1991 while touring with a mind-body-spirit conference organization.

Before her salvation, Doreen frequently appeared on Oprah, CNN, The View, Coast to Coast and other liberal secular media. After the Holy Spirit convicted her of her sins, while she read Deuteronomy 18:10-12, Doreen repented and gave her life to Jesus as her Lord and Savior. Doreen has been helping professing Christians to identify and avoid new age and new thought deception.

Doreen volunteers in discipling women who've been saved out of

New Age in a private Facebook group. Doreen was a speaker at the Answers in Genesis 2025 women's conference at the Ark Encounter. She has been featured on American Gospel 3, American Gospel TV, Daily Wire, Moody Radio, Spillover, Christianity Today, Cultish, New York Magazine, Spiritual Counterfeits Project, Servants of Grace, and other Christian media.

You can connect with me on:
- https://doreenvirtue.com
- https://x.com/doreenvirtue
- https://www.facebook.com/DoreenVirtueForJesus
- https://www.instagram.com/DoreenVirtue

Also by Doreen Virtue

Since she was saved out of the new age in 2017 and after earning her Master's Degree with Highest Honors from Western Seminary in 2021, Doreen Virtue has been warning about new age, new thought, and occult deception and pointing women to Jesus and Bible study.

Prior to her salvation, Doreen was a new age author and unfortunately some people continue to sell used and bootleg (illegally printed) copies of her old books and cards. Doreen asks that no one purchase her materials published in 2017 or earlier, and instead dispose of it.

Since 2025, Doreen only writes encouraging Christian books for Amazing Grace publishers, available through Amazon and Kindle.

Armor of God: Biblical Help for Spiritual Warfare 30-Day Devotional for Christian Women

How to Avoid New Age & New Thought Deception

Forgiving Who Hurt You
Guided Prompt Prayer Journal & Devotional to walk you through the Bible's teachings about forgiveness. Beautifully illustrated pages.

Biblical Truth about Angels
What the Bible Really Says about Angels & Archangels

Biblical Truth about Psychics
What the Bible Really Says about Pychics, Mediumship, and Divination

Praise God in the Storm
Comforting Encouraging 30-Day devotional for Christian women who are enduring hardships

Biblical Truth about Goddesses
What the Bible Really Says about Goddesses, Idolatry, and Witchcraft

 Comfort in Christ Devotional & Coloring Book

 Psalm 23 Devotional & Coloring Book

Printed in Dunstable, United Kingdom

64887766R10087